# Dinner Tonight

By Marge Perry

**For Rachel and Zachary,
who are the seasonings
in my life.**

Printed by Interstate Litho in Brentwood, N.Y.
ISBN 1-885134-185

Newsday books are available at a special discount for sales promotions, premiums, fund-raising or educational use. For information on bulk purchases, contact:

Content Development
Newsday Inc.
235 Pinelawn Rd.
Melville, N.Y. 11747-4250

Three of us put this book together. Kari Granville, food editor at Newsday, devoted innumerable evenings and weekends in order to not only help make this book the best it could be, but also get out a daily food page, a weekly food section, and handle the ongoing challenge of being a working mother. Clarke Reilly did far more than copy edit this book; her warmth, food knowledge, and genuine good humor were the bright light when deadlines loomed dark and large. Bernadette "Herbie" Wheeler, with her eagle eyes, patiently edits my daily Dinner Tonight column and makes it better.

Also at Newsday, Bob Keane, Phyllis Singer and Barbara Schuler believed in the raison d'être of this book and made it happen.

Pat Mack, food editor at The Bergen Record, is a mentor in the truest sense of the word. I will always be an apprentice to the craft she has mastered.

To my personal encyclopedia of all things food, David Bonom.

Special thanks to my supportive friends at Cooking Light magazine: Rod Davis, Nathalie Dearing, Jill Melton and Kerri Westenberg.

My family: Barbara Perry understood, opened the first door for me, and thus enabled me to do what I love every single day. Cynthia Eisen listens better than anyone I know, and shows me what readers need with her every cooking "emergency." We will always be the three Perry girls.

Jane and Bernie Perry gave me the tools to believe and strive and are always there when I falter; they are my foundation.

To my dear friends, whose love and support I cherish: Ebo, who contributed to this book in ways both great and small, Trudy and Jerry Solin, Laurie Ruckel and David Ulrich.

Rachel Emily and Zachary Aaron shared their mother with editors and phone calls and too many deadlines, and tasted and commented on every recipe in this book. Both fascinate and inspire me every day of my life.

People assume that because I develop recipes and write about food, making dinner is never an issue for me. Call it the shoemaker's children syndrome if you like, but there are many (too many) nights when I'm dashing out of my office to pick up my children and I haven't had a second to think about dinner. I know that by the time we get home, my children will be famished and they'll need my help with homework. Those are the nights I take a deep breath . . . and let it out when we all finally sit down to dinner. And I do treasure dinnertime. We talk about what happened that day, get silly, argue — the point is, we're together. Dinnertime is the foundation of our family life.

Too often, I think, dinner gets short shrift because of the pace of our lives. I, for one, simply do not have an hour to devote to making dinner. And even if I did, I often don't have the energy for it by the end of the day.

But I do want my family to eat healthful meals. And I want to give them food that delights their senses while it nourishes their bodies. Oh, and I have to like it, too, which means I'm not cooking typical kid classics like spaghetti and meatballs night after night.

The key to satisfying all these requirements is to keep the kitchen stocked with foods that do the work for you without compromising nutrition or flavor. Herbs and spices, for instance, are the easiest way to impart flavor without a lot of work. There are also some great short-cut products that taste good and have a decent nutritional profile. Cooked chicken breasts, seasoned canned tomatoes, pitted olives and pre-cut vegetables, all available in most supermarkets, cut your preparation time. Fresh fruits and vegetables don't need much to taste great. When asparagus is in season, it needs little more than a quick steam and a sprinkle of lemon juice. In the summer, ripe peaches can be sauteed with ginger and chicken breasts for an unbeatably simple, wonderful and low-fat dinner.

The recipes in this book reflect what I want to eat and feed my family on a typical weeknight. They're easy to prepare, and many were developed for the nights when I have no idea what to make for dinner until I walk into the kitchen at the end of the day.

Regardless of what I make for dinner, I always try to be sure we eat well-balanced, nutritious meals. Good nutrition is not as difficult as it may seem. Keep the right ingredients in your pantry, learn which herbs and spices most appeal to you and buy produce when it's at its best. Then, whether you're in the mood for sophisticated, interesting flavors or homey comfort foods, you can prepare a healthful, satisfying meal quickly and without fuss. Maybe you'll even have a few extra minutes to linger at the dinner table with your family.

# Dinner Tonight

# Organizing Your Pantry

*Have the right
ingredients
on hand.*

# Great meals begin here

The key to getting healthful, wonderful-tasting meals on the table quickly is a well-stocked pantry. That doesn't mean you must have a huge walk-in closet devoted to ingredients. Today, the term "pantry" refers to the combined cupboard, freezer and refrigerator.

Think about what effect your pantry has on what you eat for dinner. Unless you have time to go to the market every day, your pantry dictates what you prepare. And the way you maintain the pantry helps determine the flavors of your food.

With that in mind, you want to be sure nothing in the pantry is so old that it's lost flavor. The attractively bottled spice mixture you bought four years ago at a farmer's market may not be spoiled, but it also may not have much potency left. In fact, dried herbs and spices should be discarded after six months.

Even ingredients that don't diminish in quality shouldn't be held indefinitely. Each and every item in your pantry should be there for a reason. If you haven't used that cute bunny-shaped pasta in three years, chances are you won't any time soon. All it does is take up shelf space and make it more difficult to find the foods you do need.

Of the three components of your pantry, the freezer is easiest to organize. Use masking tape and a ball point pen to label every item you put in your freezer with the date. Put new items in the rear of the compartment and move older ones to the front to use first. That way, you won't find year-old boneless chicken breasts in the back corner when you've been buying them every week, or a cut-to-size roast that's got a good case of freezer burn and has to be thrown out.

Keep your freezer in order by grouping like foods. Frozen leftovers should be in one section, roasts in another and ready-to-use, pre-cut meat and poultry in another. Keep frozen vegetables and fruits on the door or on their own shelf, and let frozen dessert items have their special section. By maintaining the order, neither you nor other family members will have to rummage for an item and create chaos.

Follow the same concept with your refrigerator. Keep yogurt, cheese, sour cream and other dairy in one area, leftovers in another, and so on. Again, when you buy new food, be sure to put it behind what you've already got. And check your vegetable bins regularly to avoid letting that one lemon at the bottom go unnoticed.

As for organizing your cupboards, if your cabinets allow it, put your spices in alphabetical order on revolving two-tiered lazy Susans. For years, I've withstood teasing from my friends about my alphabetically ordered spice cupboard. But every night as I assemble ingredients for dinner, I experience a moment of smug pleasure when I instantly find the spice I need.

Whether in the spice cabinet or the cupboard, place all jars, cans and bottles with the labels facing outward — this is a seemingly obvious time-saver that many people don't think to do.

My dry-goods storage is organized by the way I use foods. For example, the grape jelly I use for sandwiches is kept with the peanut butter, but the currant jelly I use in cooking is next to the hoisin sauce, Worcestershire sauce and mustards.

What's more, store items according to how frequently they're needed. For instance, I keep my children's snack foods and cereals within easy reach and more infrequently used baking specialty items on top shelves.

To make dinner preparation a snap, here's what you should have on hand:

**CABINET STORAGE:**
**Canned whole beans** — A meatless, nutritious source of protein. They can be tossed in salads, used pureed or whole as the basis of soup, or cooked with a grain such as pasta or rice. Prior to using, pour beans into a strainer and

rinse under cold water. Organic beans tend to be firmer and taste less canned. Types to keep on hand are white, black and kidney beans and chick-peas as well as fat-free refried beans and low-fat baked beans.

**Dried legumes** — Split green peas and lentils both cook in less than 30 minutes and make wonderful fall and winter soups.

**Canned broth** — Lower-sodium, nonfat chicken, beef and vegetable broths are the basis of many sauces and soups, and they add subtle flavor when used to cook couscous, rice and other grains.

**Clam broth/juice**

**Canned fish** — Canned tuna and salmon, and anchovies in jars. Tuna and salmon can be used for almost-instant hot and cold dishes. Both can be served as traditional cold salads, or tossed with warm pasta, herbs and chopped tomatoes. Anchovies give depth to dressings and sauces without necessarily adding a fishy flavor. Buy anchovies in jars, not in the tins, which generally contain lower-quality anchovies.

**Rice** — Long-grain white, basmati and quick-cooking brown rices. Long-grain white rice is the most common variety used. Basmati cooks in about 15 minutes and has a pleasant, slightly nutty aroma. Quick-cooking brown rice is high in fiber and has a nutty, earthy flavor.

**Pasta** — No-boil lasagna noodles and at least one box of each shape: strand, small (such as orzo, tubetini, etc.), and large "sauce catchers" such as penne or rigatoni.

**Couscous** — This precooked grain can be soaked in boiling water, broth or other flavored liquid and be ready in about 15 minutes.

**Instant polenta** — Cooks in less than 10 minutes and can be used alone as a side dish or with sauces and beans as an entree.

**Oils** — Types to keep on hand are sesame oil, which is strongly flavored and adds an Asian touch; peanut oil, which adds nutty flavor; extra-virgin olive oil, which adds great flavor to dressings so splurge on a high-quality one from Italy, Greece or Spain, and olive oil (not extra virgin) and canola oil, healthful oils for basic sauteeing (canola has almost no flavor; olive oil adds a little bit).

**Vinegar** — Balsamic vinegar adds sweet depth, and can be used in dressings, sauces and glazes. Red wine vinegar is the most basic one for salad dressings. Rice vinegar adds sweetness to dressings and sauces and is indispensable in many Asian dishes.

**Condiments** — Salsa; hoisin sauce; low-sodium soy sauce; Asian chili paste; Tabasco; pitted kalamata olives; Worcestershire sauce; ketchup; Dijon, country Dijon and spicy brown mustards; light mayonnaise; capers; marmalade or orange fruit spread; honey and natural-style peanut butter.

**Canned tomatoes** — Whole plum tomatoes in 14½- and 28-ounce cans; diced tomatoes in 14½-ounce cans, and crushed tomatoes.

**Sauces** — Prepared spaghetti, pasta and pizza.

**Dried fruit** — Raisins, apricots and figs.

**Canned fruits** — Mandarin oranges and chunk pineapple (not in syrup).

**Herbs and spices** — My most basic herbs and spices are cumin, cinnamon, red pepper flakes, cayenne pepper, black pepper, thyme, oregano, dried mint, marjoram, rosemary, lemon pepper, bay leaves, fennel seed, chili powder, ground ginger and nutmeg. I prefer sea salt (which I believe has the purest flavor, without the edge or bite of iodized table salt) to all others, and use it in all my recipes. And although most recipes will include a specific measured amount for black pepper, I urge you to use freshly ground black pepper from a mill, which is difficult to measure so approximate the amount.

**DRY STORAGE:**

**Potatoes** — Red and baking varieties.

**Onions** — White and red.

**Garlic**

**FREEZER STORAGE:**

**Vegetables** — Chopped spinach; corn; peas; bell pepper strips; artichoke hearts; black-eyed peas and sugar snap peas.

**Fruits** — Strawberries, blueberries and/or mixed berries.

**Meat, fish and poultry** — When you're organized enough to think ahead, you can transfer meat or poultry from the freezer to the refrigerator the night before you plan to use it. Put it on a plate on the bottom shelf of your refrigerator, so that if the package leaks as it thaws, no food is contaminated.

I usually have on hand at least one package each (to serve four) of the following in my freezer: sliced pork tenderloin; boneless chicken breasts; boneless chicken thighs; flank steak; boneless, center-cut pork chops; lean ground turkey and bacon (wrapped with plastic between the slices).

In addition, I usually have the following foods, which require no forethought and can be taken from the freezer when you get home at the end of the day: shrimp (usually sold in two-pound bags); pre-cooked chicken and turkey sausage; thin-sliced, boneless chicken breasts (take them out of the package and separate them to thaw more quickly), and chicken tenderloins (again, separate them for quicker thawing).

**Bread and dough** — Prepared pizza crusts, such as Boboli; frozen bread dough (such as Bridgeford); frozen pizza dough and piecrust dough.

**Cheeses** — Grated Parmesan, shredded light mozzarella and shredded light Cheddar.

**Butter** — I generally use only 1 tablespoon of butter at a time. I wrap the remainder in plastic wrap and freeze it.

**Citrus zest** — Every time I use lemon, lime or fresh orange juice and zest in a recipe, I zest the whole fruit and freeze the extra zest in 1 teaspoon portions in plastic bags.

**REFRIGERATOR STORAGE:**

While the refrigerator stores your most perishable items, there are some items that keep up to a couple of weeks without their flavor and texture being compromised. Among the great refrigerator-keepers to have on hand are:

**Dairy products** — Feta cheese, Parmesan cheese, light sour cream, nonfat plain yogurt, buttermilk and butter.

**Produce** — Lemons, limes, celery, carrots, and green and red bell peppers.

**Breads and grains** — Ready-to-use pizza dough, ready-to-use bread and/or biscuit dough and precooked polenta.

# Chicken & Turkey

*The goodness
of fresh fruit
shines in Ginger
Peach Chicken.*

# Balsamic Glazed Chicken

## Good Idea

**COOKING:**

Pounding boneless chicken breasts to a uniform thickness helps them cook more evenly when sauteed. It prevents the problem of thinner areas drying out while the thicker areas cook. To pound breasts, place them between two sheets of plastic wrap. Place the breasts on a flat work surface and, using a meat mallet or a rolling pin, pound them until they are even, about ⅓ to ½ inch thick.

This is the kind of dish that becomes your standby chicken supper — the one you make when you don't want to think about what to cook. Everyone loves it, it's made with ingredients you're likely to have on hand, and it couldn't be easier. It's also worth noting that it gets less than 20 percent of its calories from fat.

## You Will Need

1 pound boneless chicken breasts, pounded to an even thickness
1 tablespoon Dijon mustard
1 tablespoon olive oil
2 cloves garlic, cut in thin slivers
½ cup raisins
2 tablespoons balsamic vinegar
1 tablespoon brown sugar
¾ cup nonfat chicken broth

**1.** Place the chicken breasts on a plate and spread the mustard on them. Set aside.

**2.** Heat the oil over medium high in a large, nonstick skillet. Add the garlic and cook, stirring, for 30 seconds. Add the chicken and cook until it lifts easily from the pan and is lightly browned, about 3 minutes. Turn it and cook 3 more minutes, or until browned. Remove the chicken from the pan.

**3.** Add the raisins, vinegar, sugar and broth to the pan and bring to a boil. Reduce the heat to medium, return the chicken to the pan, spoon the sauce over it and simmer, covered, for 6 to 8 minutes, or until the breasts are cooked through. Serve immediately.

**Nutritional Analysis**
For each serving: 247 calories; 27 g. protein; 23 g. carbohydrates; 1.3 g. dietary fiber; 5.2 g. fat; <1 g. saturated fat; 66 mg. cholesterol, 298 mg. sodium.

**SERVING SUGGESTION**
Serve with almond-broccoli rice: Cook 1 cup white rice according to package instructions. Add 2 cups broccoli florets to the rice during the last 5 minutes of cooking. Toss the rice and broccoli with slivered almonds, and season to taste with salt and pepper.

**SERVES 4**

# Ginger Peach Chicken

I first made this dish in the summer when I couldn't resist a whole basket of fragrant peaches, but have since discovered many fruits can be substituted. Try apples, plums or pears.

## You Will Need

1 pound boneless chicken breasts, pounded to an even thickness
½ teaspoon salt
1 tablespoon canola oil
1 tablespoon minced ginger
1 cup nonfat chicken broth
1 tablespoon honey
4 peaches, cut in ½-inch-thick slices
1 tablespoon fresh chopped basil, parsley or cilantro (optional)

**1.** Sprinkle the chicken with the salt.

**2.** Heat the oil over medium high in a large skillet. Add the chicken and cook for 5 minutes, or until it is golden brown. Turn it and cook 5 more minutes. Remove the chicken from the pan and set aside.

**3.** Add the ginger, chicken broth and honey to the pan and stir to dissolve the honey. Add the peaches, cover and cook, stirring occasionally, for 6 minutes, or until the liquid is slightly syrupy and the peaches are tender but not mushy.

**4.** Return the chicken to the pan, placing it on top of the peaches. Spoon some of the syrup over the chicken, cover and cook 3 more minutes, or until the chicken is warmed through. Garnish with chopped herb, if desired.

**Nutritional Analysis**
For each serving: 217 calories; 27 g. protein; 16 g. carbohydrates; 2 g. dietary fiber; 5 g. fat; <1 g. saturated fat; 66 mg. cholesterol, 525 mg. sodium.

**SERVING SUGGESTION**
Accompany with pignoli-nut rice: Toast pignoli nuts (pine nuts) in a dry skillet and toss while warm with extra-virgin olive oil, a pinch of sugar, salt, pepper and a pinch each of ground coriander, cayenne pepper and cinnamon. Mix with jasmine rice.

**SERVES 4**

# Chicken with Oregano, Capers and Lemon

Greek flavors abound in these sauteed breasts. The sauce, which practically happens on its own in the pan, keeps the chicken moist.

## You Will Need

3 tablespoons flour
1 teaspoon oregano
1 pound boneless chicken breasts, pounded to an even thickness
1 tablespoon extra-virgin olive oil
1 onion, cut in thin strips
3 cloves garlic, minced
1 ½ cups nonfat chicken broth
2 tablespoons lemon juice
2 tablespoons capers, divided
4 lemon wedges for garnish

**1.** Combine the flour and oregano on a plate. Dredge the chicken in the mixture, coating thoroughly.

**2.** Heat the oil in a large skillet over medium high. Add the chicken and saute 2 to 3 minutes, or until lightly browned. Turn and cook 2 to 3 more minutes. Remove the chicken from the pan and set aside.

**3.** Add the onion and garlic to the pan and cook, stirring, for 2 minutes, or until softened. Add the chicken broth, lemon juice and any remaining dredging flour, and cook, stirring and scraping bits off the bottom of the pan, for 2 to 3 minutes. Return the chicken to the pan, sprinkle with 1 tablespoon of the capers, reduce heat and simmer, covered, 5 to 6 minutes, or until the chicken is cooked through. Divide the chicken among serving plates, sprinkle with the remaining capers and serve with a lemon wedge.

**Nutritional Analysis**
For each serving: 189 calories; 28 g. protein; 7 g. carbohydrates; <1 g. dietary fiber; 5 g. fat; <1 g. saturated fat; 66 mg. cholesterol, 473 mg. sodium.

**SERVING SUGGESTION**
Accompany with orzo with feta cheese: Cook orzo al dente according to package instructions. Reserve ¼ cup of the pasta water. Drain pasta. Toss warm orzo with crumbled feta cheese, reserved cooking water and ½ teaspoon dried oregano.

**SERVES 4**

# Pizza Chicken

My daughter Rachel gave this dish its perfect name: The golden brown sauteed chicken breasts topped with tomato sauce and mozzarella really do look and taste like pizza. My children would eat this for dinner every night if they could (and so would the adults I've served it to). It's important to use very thin chicken for this — either buy the thinly sliced breasts or carefully pound regular boneless ones.

## You Will Need

1 egg
1 tablespoon skim milk
¼ cup grated Parmesan cheese
3 tablespoons flour
3 tablespoons bread crumbs
1 pound thin-sliced boneless chicken breasts
1 tablespoon olive oil
4 tablespoons tomato pasta sauce
4 tablespoons shredded light mozzarella

**1.** Combine the egg and milk in a bowl and beat lightly. Place the Parmesan cheese on a plate. Combine the flour and bread crumbs on a plate.

**2.** Dip each piece of chicken in the egg, the Parmesan, and then the flour mixture, making sure to completely coat each piece with the flour. Set the chicken aside.

**3.** Heat the oil in a large, nonstick skillet over medium high. Add the chicken and cook without moving it for 2 minutes, or until browned. Turn the chicken and cook 2 more minutes. Spread the pasta sauce over the chicken. Top with the mozzarella, cover the pan and cook 1 to 2 minutes, or until the cheese is melted. Serve immediately.

### Nutritional Analysis

For each serving: 265 calories; 34 g. protein; 9.7 g. carbohydrates; <1 g. dietary fiber; 9.2 g. fat; 3.1 g. saturated fat; 126 mg. cholesterol, 390 mg. sodium.

### SERVING SUGGESTION

Accompany with bowties and green beans: Cook farfalle pasta according to package instructions. In the last 3 minutes of cooking, add green beans to the pot. Drain and toss the pasta and green beans with halved cherry tomatoes, grated Parmesan cheese, olive oil, and salt and pepper to taste.

## Good Idea

**SAFETY:**
Chicken breasts should be cooked to an internal temperature of 160 degrees to ensure that potentially harmful bacteria have been killed. To see if a boneless breast is done, insert an instant-read meat thermometer horizontally into the center of the meat. In chicken with bones, insert the thermometer into the thickest part of the meat, being careful not to touch a bone.

**SERVES 4**

# Chicken Teriyaki

Kids and adults alike love the flavor of this slightly sweet chicken. Be sure to boil the marinade to kill off any harmful microorganisms and to concentrate the flavor before serving it as a sauce. Sometimes I double the marinade and keep the extra in the refrigerator to spoon over rice or use as a dipping sauce later in the week.

## You Will Need
3 cloves garlic, minced
1 (½-inch) piece ginger, minced
¼ cup low-sodium soy sauce
4 tablespoons rice vinegar
¼ cup honey
¼ cup water
1 pound boneless chicken breasts, pounded to an even thickness

**1.** Preheat the broiler. Line a broiling pan with foil and coat it with cooking spray.

**2.** Combine the garlic, ginger, soy sauce, vinegar, honey and water in the broiling pan and whisk until the honey is dissolved.

**3.** Place the breasts in a single layer in the broiler pan and set aside for 15 minutes to allow the chicken to marinate.

**4.** Pour off the marinade into a small saucepan and bring it to a boil. Reduce the heat and simmer for 10 minutes.

**5.** Meanwhile, broil the chicken for 6 to 7 minutes. Turn and broil 6 more minutes, checking for doneness halfway through. Divide the chicken among serving plates and serve with warm sauce spooned over the top.

### Nutritional Analysis
For each serving: 207 calories; 28 g. protein; 20.5 g. carbohydrates; <1 g. dietary fiber; 1.5 g. fat; <1 g. saturated fat; 66 mg. cholesterol, 581 mg. sodium.

### SERVING SUGGESTION
Serve with sesame-spinach rice: Rinse a handful of fresh spinach until clean. Place it in a hot skillet and toss for a couple of minutes, until it just loses its crispness and it is still bright green. Chop spinach roughly and add to white rice. Toss with sesame seeds and salt.

**SERVES 4**

# Wine-braised Chicken

This dish is inspired by the simple classic coq au vin. You need the recipe the first time or two you make it, and then you can start putting your own imprimatur on it. Change the herbs, or the vegetables, or try making it with turkey cutlets. No matter what substitutions you make, you'll end up with a lovely, thickened sauce. Serve the chicken and the sauce over egg noodles, which will absorb all the sauce, but have some bread handy just in case.

## You Will Need

¼ cup flour
½ teaspoon salt
¾ teaspoon dried thyme
1 pound boneless chicken breasts
1 tablespoon olive oil
4 carrots, cut in thin slices
2 cups sliced mushrooms
1 green pepper, cut in strips
½ cup red wine
1 cup nonfat chicken broth
1 tablespoon tomato paste

**1.** Combine the flour, salt and thyme. Dredge the chicken in the mixture.

**2.** Heat the oil in a large skillet. Add the chicken and cook until lightly browned, about 2 minutes. Turn and cook 2 more minutes. Remove the chicken from the pan.

**3.** Add the carrots, mushrooms, green pepper and any remaining dredging flour to the pan, and cook over medium-high heat for 2 minutes, or until the vegetables begin to soften. Return the chicken to the pan, add the wine, broth and tomato paste, and cook for 12 to 14 minutes, or until the chicken is cooked through. Serve the chicken with the sauce.

### Nutritional Analysis
For each serving: 259 calories; 29 g. protein; 18 g. carbohydrates; 4 g. dietary fiber; 5 g. fat; <1 g. saturated fat; 66 mg. cholesterol, 556 mg. sodium.

### SERVING SUGGESTIONS
Serve the chicken and sauce over egg noodles.

Accompany with Brussels sprouts: Trim the Brussels sprouts and remove the tough outer leaves. Cook in boiling water until just tender and drain. In the same saucepan, melt a pat of butter, add minced garlic and the Brussels sprouts and saute until the garlic is soft. Season with salt and pepper to taste.

Some crusty French bread goes nicely, too.

**SERVES 4**

# Mediterranean Baked Chicken

This dish is as easily Greek as it is Italian. The simple combination of flavors is found throughout the Mediterranean and is easily replicated with ingredients from your pantry. Cleanup is especially quick when you combine the ingredients as you go in a liquid measuring cup. And although the chicken bakes for 30 minutes, it takes only about 5 minutes to put this dish together.

## You Will Need

4 chicken breast halves on the bone, about 2 ½ pounds
¾ cup white wine
1 tablespoon tomato paste
¼ cup kalamata olives, roughly chopped
2 cloves garlic, slivered
½ teaspoon dried thyme
¼ teaspoon crushed red pepper flakes

**1.** Preheat the oven to 400 degrees. Lay the chicken breasts out in a baking dish.

**2.** Combine the white wine, tomato paste, olives, garlic, thyme and red pepper flakes, and stir until the tomato paste is dissolved. Pour the mixture over the chicken. Bake for 30 to 35 minutes, or until the chicken is cooked through. Serve the chicken with the sauce over the top.

**Nutritional Analysis**
For each serving: 389 calories; 50 g. protein; 3 g. carbohydrates; <1 g. dietary fiber; 15 g. fat; 4 g. saturated fat; 139 mg. cholesterol, 275 mg. sodium.

**SERVING SUGGESTIONS**
Accompany with lemon-parsley orzo: Toss orzo with chopped parsley, the juice and zest of 1 small lemon and grated Parmesan cheese.

Also, serve Mediterranean eggplant: Saute onion and garlic in extra-virgin olive oil until soft, add diced green pepper, peeled diced eggplant, 1 can of Italian-seasoned diced tomatoes. Cook until eggplant is soft. Season to taste with salt and pepper.

**SERVES 4**

# Caribbean Chicken

The combination of brown sugar and lime in this dish is classically Caribbean, and the spices are similar to those found in jerk chicken dishes. If you like spicy food, add a dash of cayenne pepper to the spices.

## You Will Need
1 tablespoon cider vinegar
1 tablespoon brown sugar
2 tablespoons lime juice
1 teaspoon lime zest
2 cloves garlic, minced
½ teaspoon allspice
1 teaspoon ground ginger
½ teaspoon cinnamon
½ teaspoon black pepper
1 tablespoon canola oil
1 pound thin-sliced boneless chicken breasts

**1.** Combine the vinegar, brown sugar, lime juice and zest, garlic, allspice, ginger, cinnamon and black pepper in a bowl, and set aside.

**2.** Heat the oil in a large skillet over medium high. Add the chicken and cook 2 minutes, or until the chicken is golden brown and easily lifts off the surface of the pan. Turn and cook 2 more minutes. Remove the chicken from the pan.

**3.** Pour the vinegar mixture into the pan and cook, stirring, for 2 minutes. Return the chicken to the pan, and turn once to coat it thoroughly with the sauce. Divide the chicken among plates and serve topped with extra sauce.

### Nutritional Analysis
For each serving: 176 calories; 26 g. protein; 6 g. carbohydrates; <1 g. dietary fiber; 5 g. fat; <1 g. saturated fat; 66 mg. cholesterol, 77 mg. sodium.

### SERVING SUGGESTION
Accompany with savory chile polenta: In a saucepan, saute garlic, onion and canned chopped green chiles in olive oil until soft, set aside. Cook instant polenta according to package instructions. While stirring, add in shredded light Cheddar cheese and sauteed vegetables.

**SERVES 4**

# Chicken Breasts with Remoulade Sauce

A classic remoulade sauce is made from mayonnaise flavored with mustard, capers, gherkin pickles, anchovies and herbs, and is often served with cold shellfish. I've tweaked it here — I cut the fat and gave it a pleasant tang by using yogurt as part of the base, and simplified the flavor (and the work) by reducing the number of elements in the sauce. The sauce can be doubled, with half reserved for another night when you can thin it with a little water and serve it as a salad dressing.

## You Will Need

2 tablespoons minced onion
2 tablespoons plus 1 teaspoon minced capers
¼ cup plain nonfat yogurt
2 tablespoons light mayonnaise
1 teaspoon Worcestershire sauce
1 tablespoon lemon juice
3 tablespoons flour
1 egg, lightly beaten
3 tablespoons bread crumbs
1 pound thin-sliced boneless chicken breasts
1 tablespoon olive oil

**1.** To make the sauce, combine the onion, capers, yogurt, mayonnaise, Worcestershire sauce and lemon juice in a bowl, and set aside.

**2.** Place the flour on a plate, the egg in a bowl, and the bread crumbs on another plate. Dip the chicken in the flour, then the egg, and then the bread crumbs.

**3.** Heat the oil in a large, nonstick skillet. Add the chicken and cook without moving for 2 minutes, or until it lifts easily from the pan and is lightly browned. Turn and cook 2 more minutes, or until browned. Serve the chicken with the sauce spooned over the top.

### Nutritional Analysis
For each serving: 252 calories; 30 g. protein; 11 g. carbohydrates; <1 g. dietary fiber; 9 g. fat; 1.8 g. saturated fat; 119 mg. cholesterol, 398 mg. sodium.

### SERVING SUGGESTION
Accompany with garlic and scallion mashed potatoes: Steam or microwave halved new potatoes with 2 whole garlic cloves until potatoes are very tender (to cut cooking time, use parboiled fresh potatoes sold in bags in the refrigerated case in the produce section of some markets). Remove garlic cloves, and mash potatoes with skim milk and a touch of olive oil or butter. Stir in chopped scallions.

**SERVES 4**

# Thai-inspired Curried Coconut Chicken

Be sure to use light coconut milk for this recipe — you'll get the requisite rich flavor without the additional fat. To cut back on the fat even further, you can replace up to half the coconut milk with chicken broth. The curry won't be as rich, but it will still be delicious. This dish is also wonderful when made with tofu, which absorbs the flavors of the curry and coconut more readily than chicken does. Simply cut firm tofu into ½-inch blocks and proceed with the recipe as written.

## You Will Need

1 cup jasmine rice
1 tablespoon sesame oil
1 tablespoon finely minced fresh ginger
2 teaspoons Madras curry powder
1 pound boneless chicken breasts
2 green peppers, diced
2 cups shiitake mushrooms,
   sliced (about 3 ½ ounces)
1 (14-ounce) can light coconut milk
**2 tablespoons low-sodium soy sauce**
1 tablespoon honey
⅛ teaspoon Asian chili paste,
   or more to taste

**1.** Cook the jasmine rice according to package instructions.

**2.** Heat the oil in a large, nonstick skillet over medium high. Add the ginger and curry, and cook, stirring, for 2 minutes. Add chicken, and cook for about 2 minutes, or until lightly browned. Turn chicken, add the green pepper and shiitake mushrooms, and cook 2 more minutes, or until the vegetables are softened.

**3.** Add the coconut milk, soy sauce, honey and chili sauce, bring to a boil, then reduce the heat and simmer for 10 minutes, or until the chicken is cooked through. Serve over a bed of the rice.

### Nutritional Analysis
For each serving: 478 calories; 33 g. protein; 51 g. carbohydrates; 2.5 g. dietary fiber; 14 g. fat; 6.3 g. saturated fat; 66 mg. cholesterol, 351 mg. sodium.

### SERVING SUGGESTION
Serve with wilted spinach: In a large skillet, heat a small amount of olive oil and minced garlic over medium-high heat, about 1 minute. Place cleaned fresh spinach in the pan with only the water from rinsing clinging to its leaves. Toss the spinach as it cooks and remove the pan from the heat as soon as the leaves are wilted. Add salt and pepper to taste.

## Good Idea

**QUICK DESSERT:**
Make a simple, refreshing sundae: In a parfait glass, top 2 scoops of raspberry sorbet with crushed gingersnaps and then drizzle with chocolate syrup.

**SERVES 4**

# Turkey Cutlets with Mixed Greens Salad

This is an easy, lower-fat version of the dish you find at many Italian restaurants: A breaded, fried veal chop served with chopped salad on top. Splurge on the lettuce mixture sold as mesclun mix at supermarkets; though it is costly on a per pound basis, you need very little.

## You Will Need

4 cups mixed salad greens (mesclun)
2 ripe tomatoes, cut in ½-inch dice
½ cup thinly sliced red onion
¼ cup loosely packed flat-leaf parsley
¼ cup flour
½ teaspoon salt
⅛ teaspoon pepper
2 large egg whites, lightly beaten
¾ cup bread crumbs
1 pound turkey cutlets
½ cup bottled fat-free Italian dressing

**1.** Preheat the oven to 450 degrees. Coat a cookie sheet with cooking spray.

**2.** Combine the greens, tomatoes, onion and parsley leaves and set aside.

**3.** Combine the flour, salt and pepper on a plate. Place the egg whites in a bowl. Place the bread crumbs on plate. Dredge each cutlet in the flour, then the egg, then the bread crumbs, and set aside.

**4.** Heat the cookie sheet in the oven for 2 minutes. Remove it and place the cutlets on it. Bake the cutlets for 4 to 5 minutes, turn, and bake them 5 more minutes. To serve, top each cutlet with 1 cup of the salad mix drizzled with 2 tablespoons of the dressing.

### Nutritional Analysis
For each serving: 333 calories; 32 g. protein; 29 g. carbohydrates; 2.7 g. dietary fiber; 9.5 g. fat; 2.5 g. saturated fat; 74 mg. cholesterol, 799 mg. sodium.

### SERVING SUGGESTION
Accompany with microwaved "baked" potatoes: Pierce 4 potatoes all over with a fork and wrap individually in paper towels. Arrange them in a spoke pattern in the microwave and cook on high for 12 to 14 minutes, turning once halfway through cooking (cooking times will vary according to the size of the potatoes and individual microwave ovens). Potatoes are done when they are easily pierced with a fork. To serve, split them open, fill with a mixture of light sour cream and cut fresh chives.

SERVES 4

# Chicken, Green Bean and Almond Stir-fry

This is a pleasant, light-tasting dinner that's extremely low in saturated fat. Be sure to toast the nuts in a dry pan, as the recipe states, to get the most flavor out of them. Keep a bottle of peanut oil in your pantry — it's another great way to stretch nut flavor. But if you've had yours for a while, make sure it hasn't gone bad by smelling it; nut oils don't keep as well as vegetable oils.

## You Will Need

- 1 teaspoon cornstarch
- 2 tablespoons low-sodium soy sauce, divided
- 2 teaspoons minced ginger
- 1 pound boneless chicken breasts, cut in ½-inch-wide strips
- 2 tablespoons cider vinegar
- 1 tablespoon honey
- 1 tablespoon hoisin sauce
- ¼ cup slivered almonds
- 1 tablespoon peanut oil
- ½ pound green beans, cut in 1-inch pieces
- 2 tablespoons water

**1.** Dissolve the cornstarch in 1 tablespoon soy sauce. Stir in the ginger. Add the chicken and toss to coat thoroughly. Set aside.

**2.** Combine the vinegar, honey, hoisin sauce and remaining soy sauce in a bowl, and set aside.

**3.** Heat a large, nonstick skillet or wok. Add the almonds and toast, stirring, for about 30 seconds, or until fragrant. Remove them from the skillet.

**4.** Add the oil to the skillet and heat over high for 20 seconds. Add the chicken. Cook, stirring, until lightly browned, about 5 to 6 minutes. Add the green beans and water, and cook 3 more minutes. Add the sauce and cook until slightly thickened, about 1 to 2 minutes. Stir in the toasted almonds. Serve immediately.

### Nutritional Analysis
For each serving: 260 calories; 30 g. protein; 14 g. carbohydrates; 2.9 g. dietary fiber; 9.3 g. fat; 1.3 g. saturated fat; 66 mg. cholesterol, 396 mg. sodium.

### SERVING SUGGESTIONS
Serve the chicken over a bed of quick-cooking brown rice.

Accompany with quick pickled slaw: Combine shredded carrot and cabbage (the mixture can be purchased in bags in the produce section) with rice vinegar, a pinch of sugar and a touch of sesame oil. This is best served chilled.

**SERVES 4**

# Chicken with Oranges and Feta Cheese

Feta cheese and orange complement each other beautifully in this Mediterranean-inspired dish. Be sure to remove the feta cheese from the refrigerator when you start preparing the dish so it can come to room temperature. That way, it will be sure to become slightly creamy when you toss it into the warm chicken before serving.

## You Will Need

1 tablespoon olive oil
1 medium red onion, thinly sliced
1 red pepper, diced
1 pound boneless chicken breasts, cut in strips
2 oranges, peeled and cut in 1-inch pieces
1 teaspoon orange zest
¼ cup orange juice
1 tablespoon white wine vinegar
½ cup crumbled feta cheese

**1.** Heat the oil in a large, nonstick skillet over medium high. Add the onions and peppers, and cook about 2 minutes, or until softened. Add the chicken and cook for about 3 minutes, or until lightly browned. Turn and cook 3 more minutes.

**2.** Reduce the heat to medium and add the orange pieces, zest, orange juice and vinegar, and let the mixture cook for 3 to 5 minutes. Transfer the skillet's contents to a large serving bowl or platter and gently stir in the feta. Serve immediately.

### Nutritional Analysis
For each serving: 267 calories; 30 g. protein; 16 g. carbohydrates; 3 g. dietary fiber; 9 g. fat; 3.7 g. saturated fat; 83 mg. cholesterol, 286 mg. sodium.

### SERVING SUGGESTIONS
Serve with parsley couscous and peas: Cook couscous according to package instructions, substituting nonfat chicken broth for the water. Toss with cooked peas and chopped parsley.

Accompany with steamed or braised asparagus.

**SERVES 4**

# Triple Chicken Soup

This short-cut method of making chicken soup gives you plenty of flavor on those nights when you don't have hours to let a rich stock develop. The chicken that results is tender — even the white meat doesn't dry out. An added bonus is that you get leftover chicken to use later in the week, or even freeze.

## You Will Need

3 carrots, sliced
2 parsnips (about ½ pound), thinly sliced
2 onions, chopped
4 ½ pounds chicken,
   cut into serving-size pieces
2 packets chicken bouillon (about
   5 teaspoons)
8 cups nonfat chicken broth

**1.** Place the vegetables in a large pot. Top them with the chicken and sprinkle with the bouillon. Pour in the chicken broth and bring to a boil. Immediately reduce the heat and simmer for 25 minutes, or until the chicken is cooked through.

**2.** Remove the chicken from the pot with tongs or a slotted spoon. To remove the fat, place a clean, dry paper towel on the surface of the soup. When it has absorbed as much fat as it can hold, discard the towel and repeat. Repeat this procedure as many times as it take to sufficiently skim the soup. Ladle the soup into bowls, and serve the chicken separately, or save for use later.

**Nutritional Analysis**
For each serving (soup only, no chicken): 70 calories; 2.5 g. protein; 13 g. carbohydrates; 2.1 g. dietary fiber; 1 g. fat; 1 g. saturated fat; 1 mg. cholesterol, 950 mg. sodium.

**SERVING SUGGESTIONS**
Pass a loaf of crusty French or sourdough bread and a dish of country-style Dijon mustard for the chicken, if serving.
   Serve with a green salad with sliced tomatoes dressed with a balsamic vinaigrette: 1 to 2 tablespoons balsamic vinegar, 3 tablespoons extra-virgin olive oil, a pinch of sugar or to taste, and salt and pepper to taste.

**SERVES 8**

# Chicken Burritos

## Good Idea

**QUICK START:**

For a zesty first course with a summertime meal, try quick gazpacho: Cut 4 large tomatoes, ½ small onion and 1 green pepper in large chunks. Combine them in the bowl of a food processor with 1 minced clove garlic. Pulse several times until the pieces are ¼ inch. Remove half the mixture and puree the remainder in the processor. Combine and season with salt, pepper and Tabasco sauce. Stir in ½ cup chopped parsley. Refrigerate at least 15 minutes to allow flavors to develop. Serve cold.

These burritos are slightly sweet, salty, spicy and creamy — a perfect medley of tastes and textures. And they take less than 30 minutes to get from the pantry and refrigerator to the table.

## You Will Need

1 tablespoon brown sugar
Juice of 1 large lime, divided
2 teaspoons Worcestershire sauce
1 pound boneless chicken breasts,
   cut in thin strips
1 tablespoon canola oil
1 medium red onion, cut in thin strips
3 cloves garlic, minced
1 red pepper, cut in thin strips
¾ cup chunky salsa
½ cup light sour cream
½ teaspoon cumin
½ teaspoon salt
8 low-fat, burrito-sized flour tortillas

**1.** Combine the sugar, 2 tablespoons of the lime juice and Worcestershire sauce in a large bowl. Add the chicken and toss.

**2.** Heat the oil over medium high in a large skillet. Add the onion and garlic, and cook for 2 minutes. Add the red pepper and cook for 1 minute. Add the chicken and cook for 6 minutes, stirring occasionally. Add the salsa and cook 3 more minutes.

**3.** In a small bowl, combine the sour cream, the remaining lime juice, cumin and salt.

**4.** Heat the tortillas according to package instructions. Working with 1 tortilla at a time, place ½ cup of the chicken mixture in a strip down the center, leaving 1-inch borders at the top and bottom. Top with 1 tablespoon of the sour cream mixture. Fold the top and bottom flaps in toward the center. Fold the left flap over the filling and roll the burrito closed, placing it seam side down on a serving plate.

**Nutritional Analysis**

For each serving: 569 calories; 38 g. protein; 69 g. carbohydrates; 4.3 g. dietary fiber; 14.5 g. fat; 4 g. saturated fat; 76 mg. cholesterol, 1260 mg. sodium.

**SERVING SUGGESTIONS**

Pass a bowl of extra salsa to top the burritos, along with extra sour cream mixture.

   Serve with cut raw vegetables such as carrots, celery and cauliflower florets that can be dipped in the extra salsa or sour cream.

**SERVES 4**

# Tamale Pie

I created this dinner under duress one night. I had other plans for the cooked chicken I had on hand, but as I started to prepare dinner, a "homework crisis" erupted, meaning my attention was needed elsewhere. This is a great dinner to make when you have no time to spend in the kitchen, but don't mind if something takes 30 minutes in the oven. It turned out to be a particularly kid-friendly meal because of the slightly sweet cornbread topping and the bite-size pieces of chicken. I like the fact that it is low in fat (21 percent of calories) and has a good balance of carbohydrates and protein. In addition, the leftovers re-heat well.

## You Will Need

10 ounces cooked chicken, chopped (about 2 cups)
1 (8 ¾-ounce) can creamed corn
1 (4-ounce) can mild chopped green chiles
1 (15-ounce) can kidney beans, drain and rinsed
1 teaspoon chili powder
2 tablespoons tomato paste
⅛ teaspoon Tabasco, or to taste
1 cup shredded light Cheddar cheese
1 (8 ½-ounce) box corn muffin mix
1 egg
⅓ cup skim milk

**1.** Preheat the oven to 400 degrees.

**2.** Combine the chicken, corn, chiles, kidney beans, chili powder, tomato paste and Tabasco in a 9-inch, deep-dish pie plate. Top the mixture with the cheese.

**3.** Combine the corn muffin mix with the egg and milk. Smooth the batter over the filling in the pie plate. Bake for 25 to 30 minutes, or until the crust is golden. Spoon the mixture onto plates to serve, keeping the crust intact.

**Nutritional Analysis**
For each serving: 394 calories; 28 g. protein; 50 g. carbohydrates; 8.3 g. dietary fiber; 9.3 g. fat; 2.8 g. saturated fat; 79 mg. cholesterol, 1243 mg. sodium.

**SERVING SUGGESTION**
Accompany with a "Caesar" salad: Tear romaine lettuce hearts into bite-size pieces, toss with thinly cut red onion, croutons, cherry tomatoes and a Caesar-style dressing: 1 tablespoon vinegar, ½ teaspoon Dijon mustard, 1 tablespoon extra-virgin olive oil, ¼ cup low-fat buttermilk, 2 tablespoons Parmesan cheese, 1 minced anchovy or to taste, ½ teaspoon sugar and pepper to taste.

**SERVES 6**

# Savory Sausage Bread Casserole

This bread pudding provides a homey and comforting meal and can be assembled in less than 10 minutes. Give it character by choosing one of the many specialty chicken or turkey sausages now available. My favorite for this dish is lemon chicken.

## You Will Need

6 ounces precooked chicken or
   turkey sausage, cut in ½-inch pieces
8 ounces bread, preferably stale,
   cut or torn in 1 ½-inch pieces
¾ pound tomato, diced
1 tablespoon red wine vinegar
2 cups skim milk
½ teaspoon salt
½ teaspoon fennel seeds
½ teaspoon oregano
⅛ teaspoon pepper
2 eggs, lightly beaten

**1.** Preheat the oven to 350 degrees. Coat an 8-by-8-inch baking dish with cooking spray.

**2.** Combine the sausage, bread, tomato and vinegar in a large bowl.

**3.** In a separate bowl, combine the milk, salt, fennel seeds, oregano, pepper and eggs. Pour over the sausage and bread mixture, let stand 2 minutes, then toss and let stand 2 to 3 more minutes. Transfer the mixture to the baking dish and bake for 40 minutes. Let stand 2 minutes before serving.

### Nutritional Analysis
For each serving: 333 calories; 20 g. protein; 41 g. carbohydrates; 3.6 g. dietary fiber; 9.9 g. fat; 2.7 g. saturated fat; 147 mg. cholesterol, 1006 mg. sodium.

### SERVING SUGGESTIONS
Accompany with broccoli rabe: Wash leaves and remove tough woody stems. Blanch in lightly salted boiling water. Drain, and then saute with extra-virgin olive oil and garlic. Add a squeeze of lemon juice and salt to taste.

   Also, serve broiled tomatoes: Top tomato halves with bread crumbs, salt and pepper to taste, and a drizzle of olive oil. Broil until soft.

SERVES 4

# Jambalaya

...........................................................................................................

This is one of those recipes that have a long list of ingredients but are easy to assemble. While the rice cooks, chop and saute the onion, celery, pepper and garlic. After 30 minutes, you've got an addictive jambalaya. Regulate the heat by adding more cayenne pepper at the end. But be careful — each time you add a little, be sure to toss the jambalaya thoroughly and taste before adding more.

## You Will Need

1 bay leaf
1 cup uncooked long-grain rice
1 teaspoon oil
1 onion, chopped
3 stalks celery, chopped
1 green pepper, chopped
5 cloves garlic, minced
6 ounces precooked chicken or
    turkey sausage, preferably spicy, sliced
½ teaspoon salt
1 (3-ounce) jar sliced pimientos, drained
2 teaspoons basil
⅛ teaspoon cayenne pepper
1 (28-ounce) can crushed tomatoes
10 ounces cooked chicken,
    chopped (about 2 cups)

**1.** Place 2 ¼ cups water and the bay leaf in a saucepan and bring to a boil. Add the rice, cover, and simmer over low heat for 20 minutes. Remove from heat and let stand, covered, for at least 5 minutes.

**2.** Heat the oil in a large, nonstick pan. Add the onion, celery, green pepper and garlic, and cook 3 minutes, or until the vegetables begin to soften. Add the sausage, salt, pimientos, basil, cayenne and tomatoes, and simmer for 10 minutes. Stir in the cooked rice and the chicken, and simmer 5 more minutes. Add salt and cayenne pepper to taste, and serve.

### Nutritional Analysis
For each serving: 309 calories; 20 g. protein; 41 g. carbohydrates; 5 g. dietary fiber; 7.4 g. fat; 2 g. saturated fat; 54 mg. cholesterol, 743 mg. sodium.

### SERVING SUGGESTIONS
Serve with a green salad of romaine lettuce, cherry tomatoes, thinly sliced red onion and croutons tossed with a light Dijon dressing: 1 to 2 tablespoons balsamic vinegar, 3 tablespoons extra-virgin olive oil, ½ teaspoon Dijon mustard or to taste, and salt and pepper to taste.
   Also, accompany with "jazzy" corn muffins: Use a store-bought mix for cornbread or corn muffins and mix according to package instructions. Add minced jalapeno or canned diced green chiles to taste and ¼ cup light Cheddar cheese, and mix lightly. Bake according to package instructions.

**SERVES 4**

# Moroccan-flavored Couscous

This dish takes only about 20 minutes to throw together, and less than 10 minutes to cook. The result is the exotic sweet, piquant and salty combination typical of Moroccan dishes. If you can't find apple-flavored chicken sausage, substitute another poultry sausage of your choice. Just be sure the sausage is precooked, or allow time to cook it first.

## You Will Need

¾ cup orange juice
¾ cup nonfat chicken broth, divided
1 bay leaf
1 cup couscous
1 teaspoon olive oil
2 cloves garlic, minced
2 teaspoons minced fresh ginger
1 teaspoon ground cumin
½ teaspoon salt
1 tablespoon capers, drained
½ cup raisins, preferably golden
12 ounces precooked chicken sausage,
    preferably apple flavored,
    cut in ½-inch slices
½ cup fresh cilantro, chopped
½ cup fresh mint, chopped

**1.** Combine the orange juice, ½ cup of the stock, and the bay leaf and bring to a boil. Pour in the couscous, cover and remove from the heat while you prepare the remaining ingredients.

**2.** Heat the oil in a large skillet. Add the garlic and ginger, and cook for 1 minute until fragrant. Add the cumin, salt, capers, raisins and sausage, and cook for 2 minutes. Add the remaining stock and simmer for 3 minutes.

**3.** Using a fork, scrape the couscous into the sausage mixture. Toss in the cilantro and mint, and serve immediately.

**Nutritional Analysis**
For each serving: 416 calories; 20.8 g. protein; 58 g. carbohydrates; 5 g. dietary fiber; 12.4 g. fat; 3.3 g. saturated fat; 76 mg. cholesterol, 1031 mg. sodium.

**SERVING SUGGESTION**
Serve with sauteed squash "fingers": Cut yellow and green summer squash in 2-by-¼-inch "fingers." Dredge in lightly beaten egg, then flour. Sprinkle with salt and pepper. Heat olive oil in a nonstick skillet over medium, add minced garlic and cook 1 minute. Add squash fingers and saute about 6 to 8 minutes, or until tender and golden.

**SERVES 4**

# Sausage, Bean and Kale Soup

This soup is hearty, warming peasant fare. To make this a wonderful, soul-satisfying meal, place a platter of flavorful cheese and crunchy raw vegetables in the center of the table, and be sure to get the best chewy bread you can — it's a soup made for dunking.

## You Will Need

1 tablespoon olive oil
2 chopped onions
5 cloves garlic, minced
¼ teaspoon red pepper flakes
1 teaspoon dried oregano
½ cup red wine
1 (48-ounce) can nonfat chicken broth
1 (28-ounce) can whole tomatoes, roughly chopped in their juices
1 (15-ounce) can kidney beans, drained and rinsed
1 (15-ounce) can sliced potatoes, drained
1 pound precooked chicken or turkey sausage, preferably spicy, sliced
1 pound kale, torn in 3-inch pieces
3 tablespoons red wine vinegar

**1.** Heat the olive oil over medium high in a large stockpot. Add the onion, garlic and red pepper flakes, and cook for 2 minutes. Add the oregano and wine, bring to a boil and cook for 2 minutes. Add the chicken broth, tomatoes, kidney beans, potatoes and sausage, and simmer for 10 minutes.

**2.** Working in batches, add about ⅓ of the kale to the pot and toss it until it wilts enough so that more kale can be added. Continue adding the kale in this manner, until all the kale is in the pot. This should take about 5 minutes. Stir in the vinegar and simmer 5 more minutes, or until the kale is tender. Ladle into bowls.

### Nutritional Analysis
For each serving: 350 calories; 21.6 g. protein; 38 g. carbohydrates; 11 g. dietary fiber; 12.7 g. fat; 3.1 g. saturated fat; 67 mg. cholesterol, 1439 mg. sodium.

### SERVING SUGGESTION
Accompany with garlic bread: Slice seeded semolina bread, brush the slices with olive oil and rub with a garlic clove. Sprinkle with garlic powder and a pinch of dried oregano, wrap in foil and heat.

Good Idea

**COOKING:**
To wash kale, spinach and escarole (or other greens) fill a large bowl or a clean sink with cold water. Add the greens and swirl them around with your hands. Let them sit undisturbed for a couple of minutes so the dislodged dirt falls to the bottom. Then lift the greens out of the water. Repeat this procedure, if necessary. Pat dry, if needed.

# Island Chicken, Rice and Bean "Stew"

This is one of those recipes that calls for a packaged convenience food that not only makes this dish easier, but more delicious. Check out different brands of seasoned rice and black bean mixtures to compare nutritional values if you're watching your salt or fat intake. This recipe calls for skinless, boneless chicken thighs rather than chicken breasts because thighs don't dry out as easily when cooked in liquid.

## You Will Need

1 (8-ounce) box seasoned rice and black bean mixture
2 teaspoons canola oil
1 pound boneless chicken thighs, skin removed
1 (14 ½-ounce) can stewed tomatoes
1 (8-ounce) can pineapple chunks
½ teaspoon dried rosemary

**1.** Cook the rice and bean mixture according to package instructions, omitting the oil, margarine or butter.

**2.** Heat the oil over medium high in a 2-inch-deep skillet, add the thighs and brown 3 to 4 minutes on each side. Add the tomatoes, pineapple (including the juice) and rosemary, reduce the heat to medium, cover and simmer for 7 to 8 minutes, or until the chicken is cooked through. Stir in the rice and beans, remove from the heat, cover and let stand 2 minutes, or until the rice absorbs more liquid. Serve in bowls.

**Nutritional Analysis**
For each serving: 414 calories; 30 g. protein; 56 g. carbohydrates; 6 g. dietary fiber; 6.9 g. fat; 1.3 g. saturated fat; 94 mg. cholesterol, 881 mg. sodium.

**SERVING SUGGESTION**
Accompany with a green salad of red curly leaf lettuce, thinly sliced red onion, cucumber and low-fat blue cheese dressing: ¼ cup crumbled blue cheese, ½ cup low-fat buttermilk (or to desired consistency), a splash of vinegar and plenty of freshly ground black pepper.

# Chicken Thighs Cacciatore

Cacciatore is Italian for hunter, and also the name given to stew-like dishes flavored with herbs, tomatoes, onions and mushrooms. This makes a rich stew that reheats well, so by all means, make a double batch and freeze the leftovers.

## You Will Need

8 chicken thighs, about 2 pounds, skin removed
½ teaspoon salt
¼ teaspoon black pepper
1 tablespoon olive oil
1 small red onion, diced
4 cloves garlic, minced
1 red pepper, cut in strips
1 green pepper, cut in strips
10 ounces mushrooms, cut in quarters
1 teaspoon dried thyme
½ teaspoon dried rosemary
½ teaspoon dried oregano
1 (28-ounce) can whole plum tomatoes, drained and roughly chopped
1 bay leaf

**1.** Sprinkle the chicken with salt and pepper. Heat the oil in a Dutch oven or deep skillet over medium high. Add the chicken and saute until browned, about 4 minutes on each side. Add the onion, garlic, red pepper, green pepper, mushrooms, thyme, rosemary and oregano to the pan and cook for 5 minutes, stirring. Add the tomatoes and bay leaf, reduce heat and simmer for 35 minutes, or until the chicken is cooked through. Serve in bowls.

**Nutritional Analysis**
For each serving: 322 calories; 30 g. protein; 21 g. carbohydrates; 5.1 g. dietary fiber; 14 g. fat; 3.4 g. saturated fat; 92 mg. cholesterol, 667 mg. sodium.

**SERVING SUGGESTION**
Serve with herb-stuffed bread: Roll out refrigerated bread dough and brush surface lightly with olive oil. Sprinkle with any combination of herbs: rosemary, thyme, oregano, basil, marjoram, sage. Add finely minced garlic and salt. Roll up bread, pinwheel style. Bake according to package instructions.

**SERVES 4**

# Maple-mustard Glazed Chicken Thighs

## Good Idea

### SAFETY:

Chicken thighs are cooked when they reach an internal temperature of 165 degrees. When testing for doneness, be sure you don't let the tip of the instant-read thermometer touch a bone, or you may get a false reading.

Because this maple-mustard glaze is so tasty, you really don't need to leave the skin on the thighs, and by removing it you cut out a lot of saturated fat.

## You Will Need

1 tablespoon olive oil
1 onion, chopped
2 tablespoons maple syrup
3 tablespoons country-style Dijon mustard
8 chicken thighs, about 2 pounds, skin removed
½ teaspoon salt
⅛ teaspoon black pepper

**1.** Preheat the oven to 350 degrees. Coat a baking pan with nonstick cooking spray.

**2.** Heat the oil in a small saucepan over medium heat. Add the onion and cook, stirring, for 2 to 3 minutes, or until soft. Add the maple syrup and mustard, and simmer until thick, about 2 minutes.

**3.** Sprinkle the chicken thighs with salt and pepper. Brush with the glaze and bake for 25 to 30 minutes, basting occasionally, until the chicken is cooked through. Divide the chicken among plates and serve.

### Nutritional Analysis

For each serving: 247 calories; 28 g. protein; 10 g. carbohydrates; 1 g. dietary fiber; 9 g. fat; 2 g. saturated fat; 115 mg. cholesterol, 681 mg. sodium.

### SERVING SUGGESTION

Accompany with noodles and artichokes: Cook wide egg noodles according to package instructions. Meanwhile, saute thawed frozen artichoke hearts and minced garlic in olive oil until artichokes are cooked through. Add about ¼ cup nonfat chicken broth to pan and heat. Add drained noodles and toss. Season to taste with salt and pepper.

**SERVES 4**

# Chicken Thighs with Fennel Barbecue Sauce

This is a simple year-round version of a summer favorite: barbecued chicken. The recipe calls for chicken thighs, which are more flavorful than breasts. They are lower in fat than drumsticks, but higher in fat than breasts, so they represent a compromise. To lower the fat further, remove the skin and saute the thighs in a nonstick skillet coated with cooking spray.

## You Will Need

1 teaspoon oil
1 onion, chopped
2 cloves garlic, minced
2 teaspoons fennel seeds
1 (14-ounce) can tomato puree
¼ cup nonfat chicken broth
½ teaspoon salt
¼ teaspoon red pepper flakes, or to taste
8 chicken thighs, about 2 pounds

**1.** In a medium saucepan, heat the oil over medium high. Add the onion and garlic, and cook, stirring, 2 minutes. Add the fennel seeds, tomato puree, broth, salt and red pepper flakes, and boil for 5 to 7 minutes.

**2.** Meanwhile, heat a skillet large enough to hold the chicken in a single layer over medium high. Add the chicken thighs, skin side down, and sear them until the skin is golden brown, about 5 minutes. Turn the chicken, add the sauce to the skillet, and simmer for 30 to 35 minutes, or until the chicken is cooked through. Divide the thighs among 4 plates, spoon sauce over them and serve.

### Nutritional Analysis
For each serving: 330 calories; 28.5 g. protein; 14 g. carbohydrates; 3 g. dietary fiber; 17.9 g. fat; 4.7 g. saturated fat; 94 mg. cholesterol, 808 mg. sodium.

### SERVING SUGGESTION
Accompany with orange-glazed carrots with cinnamon: Cut 5 carrots into pieces that are ¼-inch thick and 3 inches long (you should have about 2 cups). Combine in a saucepan with ½ cup of orange juice, 1 tablespoon brown sugar, ½ teaspoon cinnamon and ¼ cup water. Bring to a boil, then reduce to a simmer and cook for 12 to 15 minutes, or until tender.

**SERVES 4**

# Cheater's Chili

hili aficionados would scoff at this fast-cooked version of their beloved dish, because authentic chili, the kind that wins prizes at contests, is slow-cooked for several hours. This perfectly delicious version calls for ground turkey to reduce the fat and calories usually found in chili, but you can substitute ground beef. Sometimes, I even make a vegetarian version—I simply omit the turkey and use two cans of beans.

## You Will Need

1 tablespoon canola oil
1 onion, chopped
¾ pound lean (93 percent fat-free) ground turkey
1 tablespoon plus 2 teaspoons chili powder
1 tablespoon cumin
⅔ cup tomato sauce
1 (15-ounce) can red kidney beans, drained and rinsed

**1.** Heat the oil over medium high in a large skillet. Add the onion and cook, stirring, for 1 minute. Add the turkey and cook, stirring, for 4 minutes. Add the chili powder and cumin, cook for 1 minute, then stir in the tomato sauce and beans. Bring to a boil and cover, reduce heat to medium, and simmer for 5 minutes before serving.

### Nutritional Analysis

For each serving: 318 calories; 27 g. protein; 31 g. carbohydrates; 12 g. dietary fiber; 11 g. fat; 1.9 g. saturated fat; 53 mg. cholesterol, 337 mg. sodium.

### SERVING SUGGESTIONS

To serve, ladle chili over a bed of white rice. Top with a dollop of light sour cream or plain yogurt. Sprinkle with chopped scallions.

Accompany with a mixed green salad topped with low-fat blue cheese dressing: ¼ cup crumbled blue cheese, ½ cup low-fat buttermilk (or to desired consistency), a splash of vinegar and plenty of freshly ground black pepper. Top with crumbled baked tortilla chips in place of croutons.

**SERVES 4**

# Asian Burgers

The best way to mix ingredients with ground meat is to roll up your sleeves and use your hands. A fork, spoon or spatula makes it more difficult to distribute the ingredients evenly. Just be sure to wash your hands thoroughly with soap and water for a good 30 seconds after you've formed the patties.

## You Will Need

¼ cup hoisin sauce
¼ cup unseasoned bread crumbs
½ cup chopped red onion
½ red or green bell pepper, chopped
½ cup (4 ounces) sliced water chestnuts, drained and roughly chopped
1 tablespoon low-sodium soy sauce
1 tablespoon minced fresh ginger
1 pound lean ground turkey

**1.** Preheat the broiler and coat a baking sheet or broiler pan with cooking spray.

**2.** Combine all the ingredients in a bowl, taking care that they are evenly mixed. Shape the mixture into 6 ¾-inch-thick patties, being careful not to overwork or pack the meat.

**3.** Broil the patties for 7 minutes on each side, or until cooked through. Serve patties immediately.

**Nutritional Analysis**
For each serving: 169 calories; 17 g. protein; 12 g. carbohydrates; 2 g. dietary fiber; 6 g. fat; 2 g. saturated fat; 48 mg. cholesterol, 369 mg. sodium.

**SERVING SUGGESTIONS**
These burgers are delicious on their own, but you can serve them on hard rolls or toasted English muffins. Top with tomato, prepared horseradish and alfalfa sprouts.
Serve with sauteed snow peas: Saute thinly sliced onion, garlic and red pepper strips in 1 to 2 teaspoons sesame oil until just tender. Add snow peas and chopped water chestnuts, and cook an additional 1 to 2 minutes, or until peas are bright green and slightly softened. Remove from heat and toss with a splash each of low-sodium soy sauce and rice vinegar.

## Good Idea

**SAFETY:**
To test a burger for doneness, insert an instant-read thermometer into the center of the patty horizontally. Chicken and turkey burgers are done when they reach a temperature of 165 degrees.

**SERVES 6**

# Barbecue Turkey Burgers

The instructions in this recipe call for sauteeing the burgers. But the patties can also be broiled, which eliminates the need for the oil. Just be sure to broil them far enough away from the heat source so that the patties can cook inside before the outside burns, about 5 inches.

## You Will Need

1 pound lean (93 percent fat-free)
    ground turkey
½ onion, chopped
½ green pepper, chopped
½ cup bread crumbs
1 cup barbecue sauce, divided
1 tablespoon vegetable oil
6 slices Monterey Jack or
    Cheddar cheese (about 3 ounces)
6 sourdough or hard rolls, cut in half
6 lettuce leaves
6 thin slices red onion
6 thick slices tomato

**1.** Combine the turkey, onion, green pepper, bread crumbs, and ½ cup of the barbecue sauce in a bowl. Shape the mixture into 6 patties, being careful not to overwork or pack the meat.

**2.** Heat the oil over medium high in a large, nonstick skillet. Add the burgers and sear for 1 minute, then lower the heat to medium and cook 5 to 6 more minutes. Turn the burgers, cook 5 to 6 more minutes, then top with cheese and cook until the cheese melts and the burgers are cooked through.

**3.** Meanwhile, toast the rolls. Divide the remaining ½ cup of barbecue sauce evenly among the rolls. Place the patties on the rolls, and top with lettuce, onion and tomato to serve.

### Nutritional Analysis
For each serving: 465 calories; 26.5 g. protein; 56 g. carbohydrates; 3 g. dietary fiber; 15.4 g. fat; 4.9 g. saturated fat; 62 mg. cholesterol, 1121 mg. sodium.

### SERVING SUGGESTION
Accompany with three-bean salad: Combine steamed green beans with drained and rinsed kidney beans and chick-peas. Toss with an Italian vinaigrette made of 1 tablespoon red wine vinegar, 2 tablespoons extra-virgin olive oil, a dash each of dried oregano and thyme, ½ teaspoon sugar and salt and pepper to taste.

**SERVES 6**

# Blue Cheese-stuffed Turkey Burgers

Cooked red onion tops these rich burgers and makes a perfect sweet foil for the sharp blue cheese. To make the blue cheese easier to crumble, put it in the freezer for a few minutes beforehand.

## You Will Need

1 pound lean (93 percent fat-free) ground turkey
1 cup chopped mushrooms
1 teaspoon Worcestershire sauce
¼ teaspoon black pepper
2 ounces (about ½ cup) crumbled blue cheese
1 teaspoon olive oil
4 (½-inch-thick) red onion slices
4 hard rolls, cut in half

**1.** In a bowl, combine the ground turkey, mushrooms, Worcestershire sauce and black pepper, and mix thoroughly.

**2.** Shape the mixture into 4 balls, taking care not to overwork or pack the meat. Using your thumb, make a hole in the center of each. Place ¼ of the blue cheese in each hole. Fold meat over the cheese, completely enclosing it. Gently form each ball into a patty.

**3.** Brush the oil over the surface of each onion slice.

**4.** Coat a large, nonstick skillet with cooking spray and place it over medium-high heat. Add the burgers and onion slices to the pan. Cook the onions and burgers for 10 minutes, then turn. Cook 5 more minutes, or until the onions are soft and golden brown, and remove them from the pan. Cook the burgers 5 more minutes, or until they are cooked through. Place the patties on the rolls, top with onion slices and serve.

**Nutritional Analysis**
For each serving: 400 calories; 33 g. protein; 33 g. carbohydrates; 2 g. dietary fiber; 16 g. fat; 5 g. saturated fat; 82 mg. cholesterol, 604 mg. sodium.

**SERVING SUGGESTION**
Accompany with broccoli pasta salad: Cook bowtie-shaped pasta according to package instructions. In the last 3 minutes of cooking, add broccoli florets to the water. Drain, toss with lemon juice, extra-virgin olive oil, and salt and pepper to taste.

**SERVES 4**

# Mexicano Stuffed Burgers

Even the most hard-core food snobs I know have a secret liking of one kind of fast food or another. These fun burgers take the best flavors from Mexican fast food and combine them with the all-American burger in a healthful, universally liked dinner.

## You Will Need

⅔ cup chopped onion
1 pound lean (99 percent fat-free) ground turkey breast
½ cup drained chunky salsa, divided
1 cup shredded light Cheddar cheese
1 tablespoon canola oil

**1.** Combine the onion, ground turkey breast and ¼ cup of the drained salsa in a bowl. Shape the mixture into 4 balls, being careful to not overwork or pack the meat. Using your thumb, make a large hole in the center of each ball. Place ¼ cup of the cheese in each hole. Fold the meat over the cheese, completely enclosing it. Gently form the balls into patties.

**2.** Heat the oil in a nonstick skillet, add the burgers and cook for 7 minutes, turn, and cook 7 more minutes, or until the patties are cooked through. To serve, top each burger with 1 tablespoon of the remaining salsa.

### Nutritional Analysis
For each serving: 231 calories; 35 g. protein; 5 g. carbohydrates; <1 g. dietary fiber; 7.5 g. fat; 2 g. saturated fat; 77 mg. cholesterol, 480 mg. sodium.

### SERVING SUGGESTIONS
Serve the burgers on toasted rolls or hamburger buns with lettuce and tomato, if desired.
   Also, steam or microwave broccoli until crisp-tender. Place it in a baking dish and top with grated Parmesan and bread crumbs. Bake in a preheated 450-degree oven until topping is lightly browned.

SERVES 4

# Turkey, Bean and Cheddar Burgers

These burgers will knock your socks off, they're that delicious. And even though they include Cheddar cheese, they get only 32 percent of their calories from fat. Be sure to cut the Cheddar in fairly small dice, ¼ inch or so. This recipe makes nine patties, so freeze the uncooked ones you don't need.

## You Will Need

¾ cup diced Cheddar cheese
1 ½ pounds lean (93 percent fat-free) ground turkey
½ teaspoon salt
1 (15-ounce) can kidney beans, drained and rinsed
¾ cup bread crumbs
1 cup chopped onion
1 cup loosely packed cilantro, chopped
2 egg whites, lightly beaten
4 hamburger buns

**1.** Preheat the oven to 475 degrees. Coat a baking sheet with cooking spray.

**2.** Combine all the ingredients, except the hamburger buns, making sure they are evenly dispersed throughout the mixture. Shape the mixture into 9 1-inch-thick patties, being careful to not overwork or condense the meat.

**3.** Bake the patties for 13 to 14 minutes, or until they are cooked through. Place each patty on a bun and serve.

### Nutritional Analysis
For each serving: 361 calories; 24 g. protein; 36 g. carbohydrates; 4 g. dietary fiber; 13 g. fat; 5 g. saturated fat; 71 mg. cholesterol, 561 mg. sodium.

### SERVING SUGGESTIONS
Top the burgers with barbecue sauce, or ketchup and mustard.
   Accompany with cabbage salad: Cut cabbage into thin shreds, then across in ½-inch pieces. Combine with diced fresh tomatoes, cucumber, green olives, apple and shredded carrot. Top with low-fat blue cheese dressing: ¼ cup crumbled blue cheese, ½ cup low-fat buttermilk (or to desired consistency), a splash of vinegar and plenty of freshly ground black pepper.

**Good Idea**

**QUICK DESSERT:**
Combine several favorite flavors in one low-fat dessert by topping slices of angel food cake with sliced strawberries and bananas, and then drizzling with chocolate syrup.

# Beef, Pork & Lamb

*A hint of sweetness enlivens Steak with Caramelized Red Onion.*

# Beef Medallions with Madeira Wine Sauce

This dish works beautifully with beef tenderloin (filet mignon), which is very expensive. A less expensive alternative is eye-round cut into steaks. The meat is tasty and leaner than beef tenderloin, though not as tender.

## You Will Need

1 pound eye-round, cut into 4 steaks
½ teaspoon salt
¼ teaspoon pepper
½ cup red wine
½ cup Madeira wine
½ teaspoon tomato paste
1 clove garlic, finely minced
¼ cup finely minced shallot
½ teaspoon thyme

**1.** Season the meat with the salt and pepper.

**2.** Heat a nonstick skillet over high. Add the steaks and cook for 3 minutes, or until browned. Turn, reduce the heat to medium high, and cook 3 to 4 more minutes, or to the desired degree of doneness. Remove from the pan.

**3.** Add the red wine, Madeira and tomato paste to the pan and stir, scraping up any browned bits from the pan. Add the garlic, shallots and thyme, and reduce the heat to medium. Cook for 3 to 4 minutes, stirring frequently, or until the sauce is slightly thickened. Serve the steaks with the sauce spooned over the top.

**Nutritional Analysis**
For each serving: 222 calories; 25 g. protein; 6 g. carbohydrates; <1 g. dietary fiber; 5 g. fat; 2 g. saturated fat; 59 mg. cholesterol, 354 mg. sodium.

**SERVING SUGGESTIONS**
Serve with buttermilk mashed potatoes: Peel and dice potatoes and boil until tender (the smaller the dice, the faster they cook). Drain and combine with buttermilk, salt, pepper and a small amount of butter or extra-virgin olive oil. Mash to desired consistency. (Because buttermilk is thicker and more flavorful than regular milk, you will need less butter or oil than usual.)
    Also, accompany with steamed green beans.

**SERVES 4**

# Beef Fajitas

This beef filling is also delicious served over long-grain white rice rather than in tortillas. When serving it over rice, add some canned crushed tomatoes with the lime juice to end up with a little more sauce.

## You Will Need

1 tablespoon chili powder
2 teaspoons cumin
½ teaspoon salt
¼ teaspoon black pepper
1 pound flank steak,
   cut across diagonally into thin strips
2 teaspoons canola oil
1 red onion, thinly sliced
1 red pepper, thinly sliced
1 green pepper, thinly sliced
1 tablespoon lime juice
4 low-fat, burrito-sized flour tortillas

**1.** Combine the chili powder, cumin, salt and pepper in a bowl. Add the steak and toss.

**2.** Heat the oil in a large, nonstick skillet over medium high. Add the steak, onion and red and green peppers, and saute, stirring, about 6 minutes, or until the vegetables are soft and the steak is cooked to the desired degree of doneness. Remove from the heat and stir in the lime juice.

**3.** Meanwhile, heat the tortillas according to package instructions. Place ¼ of the meat and vegetables in a strip down the center of each tortilla, leaving a 1½-inch border at either end. Fold the bottom flap up, then roll the tortilla. Place seam side down on a plate and serve.

### Nutritional Analysis
For each serving: 477 calories; 31 g. protein; 49 g. carbohydrates; 5 g. dietary fiber; 16.9 g. fat; 5 g. saturated fat; 59 mg. cholesterol, 730 mg. sodium.

### SERVING SUGGESTIONS
Serve fajitas with several condiments: Prepared salsa, preferably green; light sour cream; chopped tomatoes, and chopped avocado or guacamole.

Accompany with Mexican vegetable rice: Cook 1 cup white rice according to package instructions. Steam 2 cups broccoli florets by adding them to rice for the last 5 minutes it cooks. Toss cooked rice and broccoli with ½ cup drained and rinsed canned black beans, 1 large chopped tomato, ½ cup chopped cilantro, and salt and pepper to taste.

**SERVES 4**

# Beef and Orange Burgundy Stew

I simply love this stew. It tastes richer than it has a right to, is hearty and satisfying, and still manages to stay within the healthful range of 30 percent calories from fat. Beef round cubes generally come in 2-inch pieces, so be sure to cut them in half or the cooking time will be off and the meat will be chewy.

## You Will Need

2 tablespoons flour
½ teaspoon salt
¼ teaspoon black pepper
1 teaspoon oregano
¾ pound beef round,
   cut in 1-inch cubes
1 tablespoon olive oil
2 carrots, thinly sliced (about 1 cup)
1 (15-ounce) jar whole boiled onions,
   drained
3 stalks celery, sliced
½ cup orange juice
½ cup red wine
½ cup nonfat chicken broth
1 tablespoon tomato paste
1 (15-ounce) can red kidney beans,
   drained and rinsed

**1.** Combine the flour, salt, pepper and oregano in a bowl. Add the beef and toss.

**2.** Heat the oil in a large Dutch oven or 2-inch-deep skillet over medium high. Add the beef and brown for 4 minutes, turn and cook for 2 more minutes. Add the carrots, onions and celery, and cook for 2 more minutes, or until the beef is browned on underside.

**3.** Add the orange juice, wine, chicken broth and tomato paste, and simmer for 20 minutes. Stir in the beans and simmer 5 more minutes, or until the beans are warmed through, then serve.

### Nutritional Analysis
For each serving: 430 calories; 28 g. protein; 43 g. carbohydrates; 12.5 g. dietary fiber; 14.4 g. fat; 5 g. saturated fat; 53 mg. cholesterol, 845 mg. sodium.

### SERVING SUGGESTIONS
Serve the stew over a bed of broad egg noodles.
   Also, accompany with steamed broccoli.

**SERVES 4**

# Quick Southwestern Beef Stew

Traditional beef stew gets a Tex-Mex twist when made with salsa and served over a bed of rice. You can pump up the southwestern flavors of this dish by topping each serving with shredded light Monterey Jack or Cheddar cheese.

## You Will Need

1 pound lean (90 percent fat-free) ground beef
1 onion, chopped
1 red pepper, chopped
1 green pepper, chopped
1 teaspoon oregano
1 teaspoon cumin
½ teaspoon salt
1 cup frozen peas
1 cup frozen corn
1 cup salsa

**1.** Heat a large skillet over medium high. Add the beef, onion and red and green peppers, and cook for 6 to 7 minutes, stirring occasionally, or until the vegetables are soft and the beef is cooked.

**2.** Pour off meat drippings. Stir in the oregano, cumin, salt, peas, corn and salsa, and cook for 5 minutes before serving.

### Nutritional Analysis

For each serving: 306 calories; 28 g. protein; 25 g. carbohydrates; 6 g. dietary fiber; 11 g. fat; 4 g. saturated fat; 41 mg. cholesterol, 700 mg. sodium.

### SERVING SUGGESTIONS

Serve stew over a bed of white rice and pass bowls of shredded cheese, chopped onion and diced tomatoes to sprinkle on top.

Accompany with a salad of romaine or curly leaf lettuce and sliced radishes dressed with light Italian vinaigrette made of 1 tablespoon red wine vinegar, 2 tablespoons extra-virgin olive oil, a dash of dried oregano and ½ teaspoon sugar.

## Good Idea

**SHOPPING:**
Read the nutrition label on jars of salsa. They vary greatly in both fat and sodium content, and some of the lowest fat salsas are among the most tasty.

**SERVES 4**

# Dry-rubbed Steak

Flank steak is one of the most flavorful — and leanest — cuts of meat and is ideally suited to grilling or broiling. Be sure to let it rest before slicing it thinly and diagonally across the grain.

## You Will Need

2 teaspoons chili powder
2 teaspoons garlic powder
1 teaspoon cumin
2 teaspoons brown sugar
½ teaspoon salt
¼ teaspoon ground black pepper
1 pound flank steak

**1.** Coat a broiling pan with cooking spray and preheat the broiler.

**2.** Combine the chili powder, garlic powder, cumin, sugar, salt and pepper. Rub the mixture over the surface of the meat.

**3.** Broil the steak for 5 to 7 minutes on each side, or to desired degree of doneness. Let the meat stand for 5 minutes and slice very thinly across the grain to serve.

**Nutritional Analysis**
For each serving: 200 calories; 24 g. protein; 4 g. carbohydrates; <1 g. dietary fiber; 9 g. fat; 4 g. saturated fat; 59 mg. cholesterol, 378 mg. sodium.

**SERVING SUGGESTIONS**
Accompany with parsley potatoes: Cut 1 pound new potatoes into ¼-inch wedges, place in a saucepan and cover with cold water. Bring to a boil and simmer until tender, 15 to 20 minutes. Drain and toss with 1 tablespoon olive oil, chopped parsley and salt and pepper.

Also, serve broiled tomatoes: Cut off the top ⅛ of each tomato. Gently squeeze them as you would a lemon to expel some of the seeds. Slice a small piece off bottoms so tomatoes will sit on a flat surface. Spread 1 tablespoon of seasoned bread crumbs evenly over the top surface of each tomato and drizzle with 1 teaspoon olive oil. Broil until tender and lightly browned.

**SERVES 4**

# Steak with Caramelized Red Onion

This makes a good old-fashioned steak dinner that's enlivened with the addition of caramelized onion. If some of your family members or guests like their meat medium-rare and others prefer it more well-done, pan frying is the best way to satisfy everyone. Cook the steak to medium rare, remove it from the pan, let it rest and cut it into strips. Toss some of the strips back into the hot skillet to cook them for another minute or two, stirring constantly. You needn't add more oil to the pan, and don't leave the strips in until they curl up or they'll be tough.

## You Will Need
1 tablespoon olive oil
1 red onion, thinly sliced
1 teaspoon sugar
1 teaspoon dried thyme
1 tablespoon balsamic vinegar
1 pound flank steak
½ teaspoon salt
⅛ teaspoon pepper

**1.** Heat the oil in a large, nonstick skillet over medium high. Add the onion, and cook for 4 minutes, or until softened and partially browned. Add the sugar, thyme and balsamic vinegar, and cook 5 more minutes. Remove the onion.

**2.** Sprinkle the steak with the salt and pepper. Add it to the pan and cook for 5 to 7 minutes on each side, or to desired degree of doneness. Transfer to a cutting board and let rest 3 to 5 minutes. To serve, cut the steak diagonally across the grain into very thin (¼-inch) strips. If you wish, return some of the pieces to the pan for further cooking. Serve the meat fanned out on the plate and top with the onions.

**Nutritional Analysis**
For each serving: 237 calories; 24 g. protein; 6.4 g. carbohydrates; <1 g. dietary fiber; 12.3 g. fat; 4.4 g. saturated fat; 59 mg. cholesterol, 366 mg. sodium.

**SERVING SUGGESTIONS**
Accompany with steamed green beans.
Also, serve sauteed golden potatoes: Heat 1 tablespoon canola oil in a nonstick skillet. Add 3 cups frozen diced potatoes (often labeled hash browns, but containing no added fat) and 1 cup shredded carrot. Cook, breaking up frozen chunks, for about 10 minutes, or until the potatoes are browned and tender. Add salt and plenty of pepper to taste.

**SERVES 4**

# Warm Skirt Steak, Green Bean and Potato Salad

Skirt steak is a tasty, rich cut of meat. It is best served cut in strips, as in this recipe, or in fajitas. It is higher in fat than flank steak, which can also be used in this recipe, but has a unique, particularly robust flavor. The nutritional analysis below is approximate: the USDA has no official numbers for skirt steak.

## You Will Need

1½ pounds unpeeled red potatoes, cut into ½-inch dice
1¼ pounds green beans
1 pound skirt steak
½ teaspoon salt
1 tablespoon balsamic vinegar
1 tablespoon plus 2 teaspoons orange juice
½ cup parsley, chopped

**1.** Preheat the broiler and coat the broiling pan with cooking spray.

**2.** Combine the potatoes with enough cold water to cover them by 3 inches in a saucepan. Bring the water to a boil and cook the potatoes about 8 minutes or until crisp-tender. Add the green beans and cook 5 more minutes, or until they are bright green and slightly crisp.

**3.** Meanwhile, broil the skirt steak about 5 minutes on each side, or until nicely browned on the exterior but still red in the center. Cut the steak across into ¼-inch-thick strips.

**4.** In a large bowl, combine the salt, vinegar and orange juice. Toss in the potatoes, beans, steak and parsley. Serve warm.

### Nutritional Analysis
For each serving: 359 calories; 29 g. protein; 33 g. carbohydrates; 8 g. dietary fiber; 12 g. fat; 5 g. saturated fat; 58 mg. cholesterol, 384 mg. sodium.

### SERVING SUGGESTION
Serve with sliced cantaloupe as a first course.

SERVES 4

# Beefy Stuffed Potatoes

These hearty potatoes are low in fat, despite a rich beef filling and cheese topping. I often have a little of the beef left over for a Sloppy Joe-style sandwich the next day.

## You Will Need

4 baking potatoes
1 pound lean (90 percent fat-free) ground beef
1 onion, chopped
1 green pepper, diced
1 cup barbecue sauce
8 tablespoons (½ cup) shredded light Cheddar cheese

**1.** Wash and dry the potatoes and pierce them in several places with a fork. Wrap the potatoes individually in dry paper towels and set them in a spoke pattern on a plate. Microwave on high for 12 to 14 minutes, or until they are tender but not completely soft.

**2.** Remove the potatoes from the microwave and cut in half. Leaving a ½-inch border, scoop out the flesh, taking care not to tear the skin. Chop the flesh into ½-inch pieces and set aside with the skins.

**3.** Meanwhile, in a large, nonstick skillet, combine the beef, onion and green pepper, and cook over medium heat for 6 minutes, stirring to crumble the beef as it cooks. Stir in the barbecue sauce and potato flesh, and cook 2 to 3 minutes.

**4.** Fill the potato skins with the beef and potato mixture, allowing the filling to mound on the top. To serve, sprinkle each potato half with 1 tablespoon of the cheese and microwave for 1 minute, or until the cheese is slightly melted.

### Nutritional Analysis
For each serving: 443 calories; 33 g. protein; 45 g. carbohydrates; 5 g. dietary fiber; 15 g. fat; 6 g. saturated fat; 51 mg. cholesterol, 620 mg. sodium.

### SERVING SUGGESTION
Serve with a salad of Bibb lettuce, sliced radishes and alfalfa sprouts dressed with a light Dijon vinaigrette: 1 to 2 tablespoons balsamic vinegar, 3 tablespoons extra-virgin olive oil, ½ teaspoon Dijon mustard or to taste, and salt and pepper to taste.

**SHOPPING:**
Ground beef is available with varying levels of fat. For some recipes, where the beef is mixed with liquid such as tomato sauce, you can use the leanest available. But bear in mind that a burger is moist and flavorful when made with ground beef with a slightly higher fat content.

# Spice-rubbed Lamb Chops

A friend made these lamb chops for me and I was hooked. Using the shoulder blade, rather than the classic rib, gives a dinner of lamp chops a whole different feel. For one thing, you end up with a thin but sizeable piece of meat on your plate, which seems like a treat (even though you're eating less than 4 ounces). Although they are thinner, shoulder chops remain tender and flavorful when you cook them to the medium-rare stage.

## You Will Need

3 tablespoons tomato paste
1 teaspoon ground coriander
½ teaspoon cinnamon
½ teaspoon ground ginger
½ teaspoon salt
⅛ teaspoon pepper
4 shoulder lamb chops,
    about 1½ pounds

**1.** Preheat the broiler. Coat a broiler pan with cooking spray.

**2.** Combine the tomato paste, coriander, cinnamon, ginger, salt and pepper. Using the back of a spoon, rub the mixture over the surface of the lamb chops. Broil the lamb chops for 4 to 6 minutes on each side, or until they are medium-rare and still tender. Serve immediately.

**Nutritional Analysis**
For each serving: 285 calories; 25 g. protein; 3 g. carbohydrates; <1 g. dietary fiber; 19 g. fat; 8 g. saturated fat; 94 mg. cholesterol, 374 mg. sodium.

**SERVING SUGGESTIONS**
Accompany with quick-cooking barley: Cook barley according to package instructions, adding a bay leaf and golden raisins to the pot. Remove the bay leaf when barley is cooked. Toss with salt, pepper, chopped cilantro and lemon juice. (Read package labels carefully. Quick-cooking barley is ready to eat in about 15 minutes. Traditional barley cooks very slowly.)

Also, serve butternut squash: Peel squash and cut in ½-inch dice. Boil until tender and mash with a fork or potato masher. Mix with a drizzle of honey and a touch of cayenne pepper.

**SERVES 4**

# Lamb Kebabs

Don't be put off by the long list of ingredients in this recipe — most are sitting in your spice cabinet. This is quite an easy dish to assemble and cook. One note: If you have dried apricot halves rather than whole, put two together on the skewer — if the fruit is too thin it burns.

## You Will Need

4 teaspoons dried mint
½ teaspoon cinnamon
¼ teaspoon nutmeg
1 teaspoon cumin
⅛ teaspoon cayenne pepper
½ teaspoon salt
3 cloves garlic, minced
2 teaspoons extra-virgin olive oil
1 pound boneless leg of lamb,
   cut into 1½-inch pieces
12 dried whole apricots
2 red onions, each cut in 8 pieces
1 red pepper, cut in 1½-inch pieces
1 green pepper, cut in 1½-inch pieces

**1.** Preheat the broiler. Coat a broiler pan with cooking spray.

**2.** Combine the mint, cinnamon, nutmeg, cumin, cayenne, salt, garlic and olive oil in a bowl. Add the lamb and apricots, and toss thoroughly.

**3.** To prepare the kebabs, place an onion at the end of each skewer, then alternate the lamb, red and green pepper and apricots. Repeat until all the skewers are full and all the ingredients have been used. Pour any remaining liquid over the kebabs.

**4.** Lay the kebabs on the broiling pan. Place them about 5 inches from the heat and broil for 5 minutes. Turn the skewers and broil 5 more minutes. Serve immediately.

**Nutritional Analysis**
For each serving: 264 calories; 25 g. protein; 22 g. carbohydrates; 4 g. dietary fiber; 9 g. fat; 2.6 g. saturated fat; 73 mg. cholesterol, 352 mg. sodium.

**SERVING SUGGESTION**
Serve with couscous cooked with chopped sun-dried tomatoes in chicken broth and then tossed with fresh chopped parsley.

**SERVES 4**

# Middle Eastern Lamb Stew

## Good Idea

**FREEZING:**

Stews tend to freeze well, and most can be reheated without thawing. Simply place the frozen stew in a saucepan over low heat and cover it, remembering to stir or turn it over so it defrosts and heats evenly. If you're adding rice, pasta or precooked beans, add it at the last minute.

If you prefer, substitute 1 pound of ground lamb for the cubed lamb in this recipe — just omit the flour. If you've never used canned butter beans before, you're in for a pleasant surprise. They have a creamy texture and slightly nutty flavor — and the healthful nutritional profile you expect from beans.

## You Will Need

1 cup elbow macaroni
1½ pounds lamb shoulder chop, trimmed of visible fat and cut in ¾-inch cubes
1 tablespoon flour
1 tablespoon olive oil
1 onion, diced
1 cup frozen sliced carrots
2 teaspoons dried oregano
¼ teaspoon allspice
½ teaspoon salt
½ cup red wine
½ cup orange juice
1 (14-ounce) can diced tomatoes
1 (15-ounce) can butter beans, drained and rinsed

**1.** Cook the elbow macaroni until al dente according to package instructions. Drain and set aside.

**2.** Toss the lamb with the flour. Heat the oil in a large, deep skillet, add the onion and carrot and cook for 2 minutes. Add the oregano, allspice, salt and lamb and cook for 5 minutes, stirring occasionally, until the lamb is browned on all sides. Add the wine and stir, scraping up brown bits from the bottom of the pan. Add the orange juice and tomatoes, and simmer for 10 minutes.

**3.** Stir in the butter beans and macaroni and cook 4 to 5 more minutes, or until heated through. Serve immediately.

**Nutritional Analysis**

For each serving: 560 calories; 40 g. protein; 56 g. carbohydrates; 7 g. dietary fiber; 16 g. fat; 5 g. saturated fat; 100 mg. cholesterol, 960 mg. sodium.

**SERVING SUGGESTIONS**

Accompany with a salad of shredded lettuce, thinly sliced red onion, thinly sliced green and red peppers, grated cucumber and fresh dill. Dress with a lemon vinaigrette: 1 tablespoon lemon juice, 2 tablespoons extra-virgin olive oil, a pinch of sugar, and salt and pepper to taste.

Also, serve with sourdough rolls or bread.

**SERVES 4**

# Sesame Hoisin Pork and Broccoli

This is a stir-fry that hardly requires any chopping or assembling of ingredients. It's so easy that it can be on the table 15 minutes after you walk in the door. Use this recipe as a basic blueprint, but try the following alterations as time and ingredients allow:

✱ Saute 1 teaspoon of fresh minced ginger and 2 minced garlic cloves for 30 seconds before adding the pork.
✱ Replace the pork with chicken or turkey. Also, pork tenderloin works just as well as the center-cut chops.
✱ Replace the broccoli with cauliflower, but allow an extra minute or 2 for cooking.
✱ Toss in any leftover cooked vegetables in the last 2 minutes of cooking—just long enough to warm and coat them with the sauce.

## You Will Need

1 pound boneless center-cut pork chops, cut across into ¼-inch-thick strips
½ cup hoisin sauce, divided  4 PTS
1 tablespoon sesame oil     4 PTS
1 pound broccoli crowns, cut into florets (about 7 to 8 cups)
½ cup water
2 tablespoons sesame seeds  2 PTS

**1.** Toss the pork with ¼ cup of the hoisin.

**2.** In a large skillet with a lid, heat the oil over medium high. Add the pork and cook for 3 to 4 minutes, or until cooked through. Remove the pork from the pan with a slotted spoon or tongs. Place the broccoli and water in the skillet and toss thoroughly. Cover the pan and steam the broccoli for about 4 minutes, or until just tender and bright green.

**3.** Return the pork to the pan with the remaining ¼ cup of hoisin, toss thoroughly and cook for about 2 minutes, or until the pork is warmed through. Stir in the sesame seeds and serve immediately.

### Nutritional Analysis
For each serving: 365 calories; 28 g. protein; 21 g. carbohydrates; 5 g. dietary fiber; 19 g. fat; 5.3 g. saturated fat; 67 mg. cholesterol, 598 mg. sodium.

### SERVING SUGGESTION
As a first-course, serve wedges of melon sprinkled with salt and lemon juice.
   Serve the stir-fry over white rice tossed with chopped peanuts.

**SERVES 4**

# Honey Mustard Pork Chops

When buying pork chops on the bone, bear in mind that thinner ones work best for a fast, easy dinner. Thick chops must be braised in liquid or baked to cook through, while thinner chops can be simply sauteed, as in this recipe.

## You Will Need

4 lean bone-in pork chops, about 1½ pounds
½ teaspoon salt
⅛ teaspoon pepper
1 tablespoon canola oil
1 onion, chopped
1 cup nonfat chicken broth
1 tablespoon Dijon mustard
1 tablespoon honey

**1.** Season the pork chops with the salt and pepper. Heat the oil over medium high in a skillet large enough to hold the pork chops in a single layer without crowding. Add the pork and cook for 6 minutes, or until browned, turn and cook 5 to 6 more minutes. Transfer the chops to a plate.

**2.** Add the onion to the skillet and cook 2 minutes. Add the broth and boil for 3 minutes, or until the liquid is reduced by about a third. Stir in the mustard and honey, and boil, stirring occasionally, for 3 more minutes.

**3.** Return the pork to the pan for 1 to 2 minutes, turning once to coat with the sauce and warm through. To serve, spoon the sauce and onions over the chops.

### Nutritional Analysis
For each serving: 246 calories; 27 g. protein; 9 g. carbohydrates; <1 g. dietary fiber; 11 g. fat; 3 g. saturated fat; 75 mg. cholesterol, 601 mg. sodium.

### SERVING SUGGESTIONS
Accompany with orzo and spinach: Cook orzo according to package instructions. About halfway through cooking, add 1 (10-ounce) box frozen chopped spinach. Drain and season with salt, pepper and a dash of nutmeg.

Also, serve boiled or microwaved baby-cut carrots tossed with a splash of orange juice and salt.

**SERVES 4**

# Maple Pecan Pork Chops

My kids love the sweet, nutty flavor of this dish as is, but a Jamaican friend adds a little hot sauce to hers to give it a flavor more reminiscent of jerk seasoning. It's great either way, so I just pass the hot sauce at the table.

## You Will Need

1 tablespoon olive oil
1 pound boneless center-cut pork chops
¼ cup apple juice
2 teaspoons Dijon mustard
¼ teaspoon ground ginger
2 tablespoons maple syrup
¼ cup pecans, lightly chopped

**1.** Heat the oil in a large skillet over medium high. Add the pork chops and cook, without moving, for 3 minutes, or until they are browned and lift readily from the pan. Turn and cook 3 more minutes.

**2.** Meanwhile, in a small bowl, mix together the apple juice, mustard, ginger and maple syrup. When the chops have seared on both sides, add the apple juice mixture to the pan. Turn the heat to medium and stir, scraping any bits off the bottom of the pan. Simmer for 5 minutes.

**3.** Add the pecans to the pan, simmer 2 to 3 more minutes, turning the chops once to coat with the sauce. Serve immediately, spooning the sauce and nuts over the chops.

**Nutritional Analysis**
For each serving: 254 calories; 22 g. protein; 16 g. carbohydrates; 4.7 g. dietary fiber; 11 g. fat; 2 g. saturated fat; 124 mg. cholesterol, 839 mg. sodium.

**SERVING SUGGESTION**
Accompany with grated zucchini and potato: Grate ¾ pound zucchini, ½ large onion and 1 large washed but unpeeled potato. Heat 1 tablespoon extra-virgin olive oil over medium high in a nonstick skillet. Add zucchini mixture and cook, stirring, 1 minute. Add ¼ teaspoon nutmeg, ½ teaspoon salt and 1 cup nonfat chicken broth, and cook, stirring occasionally, for 10 to 12 minutes, or until the mixture begins to dry out and thicken slightly.

**SERVES 4**

# Orange Ginger Pork Stir-fry

This simple, sweet and pungent stir-fry cooks in about 10 minutes. Just be sure you have all your ingredients cut and measured before you start cooking.

## You Will Need
3 tablespoons orange fruit spread
3 tablespoons orange juice
3 tablespoons low-sodium soy sauce
2 teaspoons canola or peanut oil
¾ pound pork tenderloin,
    cut in 1½-by-½-inch strips
1 tablespoon plus 1 teaspoon
    grated ginger, divided
1 medium zucchini,
    cut in 1½-by-½-inch strips
2 medium red peppers,
    cut in 1½-by-½-inch strips
2 teaspoons cornstarch dissolved
    in 2 tablespoons water

**1.** Combine the fruit spread, orange juice and soy sauce in a small bowl, and stir to dissolve the fruit spread.

**2.** Heat the oil over medium high in a nonstick skillet, add the pork and cook, stirring, for 3 minutes. Add 1 tablespoon of the ginger and cook 30 seconds. Remove the pork from the pan.

**3.** Add the zucchini and red peppers to the pan and cook, stirring, for 3 minutes. Stir in the pork and cook 1 minute. Add the orange and soy mixture and the remaining 1 teaspoon of ginger and cook, stirring, for 1 minute. Add the cornstarch mixture and cook for 2 more minutes, stirring until the sauce is thickened and shiny. Serve immediately.

**Nutritional Analysis**
For each serving: 225 calories; 27 g. protein; 14 g. carbohydrates; 2.3 g. dietary fiber; 7 g. fat; 2 g. saturated fat; 67 mg. cholesterol, 446 mg. sodium.

**SERVING SUGGESTION**
Serve over white rice for a nutritionally complete meal.

**SERVES 4**

# Polynesian Pork

Bottled plum sauce is too sweet to use on its own, but it's perfect when balanced with lemon and soy sauce. This sauce is ideal for basting grilled meat and poultry, or adapting to any combination of vegetables and meats in a stir-fry.

## You Will Need

1 pound pork tenderloin,
   cut in ½-inch cubes
1 tablespoon sherry
3 tablespoons low-sodium
   soy sauce, divided
½ cup plum sauce
2 tablespoons plus 1 teaspoon
   lemon juice
1 teaspoon peanut or canola oil
1 tablespoon minced ginger
1 green pepper, cut in ½-inch dice
1 red pepper, cut in ½-inch dice
1 medium yellow squash,
   about ½ pound, cut in ½-inch dice
1 tablespoon cornstarch dissolved
   in 2 tablespoons water

**1.** Toss the pork with the sherry and 1 tablespoon of the soy sauce and set aside.

**2.** In a small bowl, combine the remaining 2 tablespoons of soy sauce, plum sauce and lemon juice.

**3.** Heat the oil in a nonstick skillet over medium high, add the pork and cook for 3 minutes. Add the ginger and cook 30 seconds. Remove the pork from the pan.

**4.** Add the peppers and squash to the pan and cook, stirring, for 3 minutes. Add the pork, stir, then add the sauce and cook for 1 minute. Add the cornstarch mixture and cook for 2 minutes, stirring until the sauce is thickened and shiny, then serve.

**Nutritional Analysis**
For each serving: 244 calories; 26 g. protein; 21 g. carbohydrates; 2.6 g. dietary fiber; 6 g. fat; 2 g. saturated fat; 67 mg. cholesterol, 1099 mg. sodium.

**SERVING SUGGESTION**
Serve over noodles such as vermicelli or linguine for a complete meal.

**SERVES 4**

# Pork Chops with Mustard Rosemary Sauce

## Good Idea

**SAFETY:**

My mother used to say "you can't be too careful with pork." Today the incidence of trichinosis in pork is much lower than it was. The parasite is killed off at 137 degrees, and the USDA recommends cooking pork to 160 degrees to prevent other food-borne illnesses. However, pork gets tough when overcooked even a little, so it's especially important to use a meat thermometer to determine when pork has just reached 160 degrees. It is safe to eat when slightly pink at the center.

Make these chops for dinner once and you'll make them over and over again. They're proof that sometimes the simplest preparation with very few ingredients yields crowd-pleasing results.

## You Will Need

4 lean bone-in pork chops, about 1½ pounds
½ teaspoon salt
⅛ teaspoon pepper
1 tablespoon oil
½ small onion, chopped
¾ cup nonfat chicken broth
1 tablespoon Dijon mustard
1 teaspoon dried rosemary
Pepper to taste

**1.** Season the pork with the salt and pepper.

**2.** Heat the oil in a nonstick skillet over medium high. Add the pork and cook 7 minutes on each side, or until browned on the outside and cooked through. Transfer to a plate and keep warm.

**3.** Add the onion to the pan and cook for 3 minutes. Add the chicken broth and boil about 3 minutes, or until reduced by about a third. Stir in the mustard, rosemary and pepper to taste. Pour the sauce over the pork and serve.

**Nutritional Analysis**
For each serving: 200 calories; 25 g. protein; 2.7 g. carbohydrates; <1 g. dietary fiber; 9.4 g. fat; 2.4 g. saturated fat; 70 mg. cholesterol, 579 mg. sodium.

**SERVING SUGGESTIONS**
Accompany with mushrooms and noodles: Saute any combination of sliced mushrooms (button, shiitake, Portobello, cremini) in olive oil, garlic and a splash of balsamic vinegar until soft. Add diced tomatoes, cook 3 to 4 minutes and toss with broad egg noodles.

Also, serve with Brussels sprouts: Peel any discolored outer leaves off the Brussels sprouts and make an X in the core with a paring knife. Place in lightly salted boiling water until brightly colored and fork tender (but not mushy). Drain and toss with 1 tablespoon of butter and a squeeze of lemon juice.

# Quick Roast Pork Tenderloin

Tenderloin is a very lean cut of pork that usually weighs about a pound. After the shrinkage that occurs during cooking, it will yield about four 3-ounce servings — 3 slices of meat fanned out on each plate.

## You Will Need

1 pound pork tenderloin
1 tablespoon country-style Dijon mustard
1 tablespoon orange marmalade
½ teaspoon salt
¼ teaspoon pepper

**1.** Preheat the oven to 450 degrees. Coat a baking dish with cooking spray.

**2.** Make a slit lengthwise down the center of the tenderloin, cutting about ¾ of the way through the meat. Open up the tenderloin as you would a book.

**3.** In a small bowl, mix together the mustard and marmalade. Spread the mixture along the inside cut surface of the tenderloin. Fold the tenderloin back together. Use kitchen string to tie the tenderloin together so that it keeps its shape during cooking.

**4.** Sprinkle the outside surface with the salt and pepper. Place the tenderloin in the prepared baking dish and roast for 20 minutes. Remove from the oven. Let the meat rest 5 minutes, then cut it on a slight diagonal into 1-inch-thick slices. Remove the kitchen string and serve.

**Nutritional Analysis**
For each serving: 156 calories; 24 g. protein; 4 g. carbohydrates; 0 dietary fiber; 4 g. fat; 1 g. saturated fat; 67 mg. cholesterol, 431 mg. sodium.

**SERVING SUGGESTIONS**
Accompany with small cooked shells tossed with shredded light mozzarella, a generous amount of chopped parsley, extra-virgin olive oil, salt and pepper.
   Also, serve carrots and onions: Cook baby carrots until almost tender, add in frozen baby onions. Drain and toss with 1 to 2 teaspoons butter, a pinch of cumin, salt and pepper.

**SERVES 4**

# Pork Chops with Apple, Fennel and Red Onion

This German-style dish has a subtle sweet-and-sour flavor. Use Golden Delicious apples for their texture and sweetness, or Granny Smith, which are more tart and also hold up well to cooking.

## You Will Need

1 pound boneless center-cut pork chops
½ teaspoon salt
⅛ teaspoon pepper
1 teaspoon canola oil
1 red onion, thinly sliced
1 small bulb fennel, thinly sliced
1 tablespoon plus 1 teaspoon
  apple cider vinegar
1 teaspoon sugar
2 medium apples, peeled and
  thinly sliced
1 cup nonfat chicken broth
1 tablespoon Dijon mustard

**1.** Season the pork chops with the salt and pepper. Heat the oil in a nonstick skillet over medium high. Add the pork and sear 3 minutes on each side, or until browned and chops lift readily from the pan. Remove the pork from the pan.

**2.** Add the onion and fennel to the pan and cook 3 to 4 minutes, or until softened and slightly golden. Add the vinegar, sugar, apples, chicken broth and mustard, and stir to combine thoroughly. Return the pork to the pan, reduce the heat to medium, cover, and cook for 5 to 6 minutes, or until the pork is cooked through. Serve with the apple-fennel mixture spooned over the pork.

**Nutritional Analysis**
For each serving: 268 calories; 27 g. protein; 20 g. carbohydrates; 4.5 g. dietary fiber; 9 g. fat; 3 g. saturated fat; 62 mg. cholesterol, 629 mg. sodium.

**SERVING SUGGESTIONS**
Serve with broad egg noodles tossed with light sour cream and salt.
   Accompany with butternut squash: Peel squash with a vegetable peeler and cut into ¾-inch cubes. Cook in lightly salted boiling water for about 12 minutes, or until soft. Drain and mash with skim milk, a pinch of allspice, a dash each of cinnamon and nutmeg, and salt and pepper to taste.

**SERVES 4**

# Pork Chops with Dried Cherry Sauce

Dried cherries were once a specialty store item, but now they're available at most supermarkets. They make a great alternative to raisins in baked goods, and they provide a sweet, rich flavor base for a sauce to serve with pork, beef and chicken. They are also delicious as a snack.

## You Will Need

½ cup apple juice
½ cup red wine
1 tablespoon sugar
¼ cup dried cherries
2 teaspoons raspberry vinegar
¼ teaspoon ground ginger
4 lean bone-in pork chops,
   about 1½ pounds
½ teaspoon salt
¼ teaspoon pepper
2 teaspoons canola oil
2 teaspoons cornstarch
   dissolved in 1 tablespoon water

**1.** Combine the apple juice, red wine, sugar, cherries, vinegar and ginger in a small bowl and set aside.

**2.** Season the pork chops with the salt and pepper. Heat the oil in a nonstick skillet over medium high. Add the pork and sear 3 minutes on each side, or until browned and the chops lift readily from the pan. Reduce the heat to medium and add the apple juice mixture to the pan. Cook 6 to 7 more minutes, or until the pork is cooked through. Remove the chops from the pan and stir in the cornstarch. Bring the sauce to a boil, and cook, stirring, until thickened. Serve the chops with the sauce spooned over them.

### Nutritional Analysis
For each serving: 251 calories; 24 g. protein; 14 g. carbohydrates; <1 g. dietary fiber; 8 g. fat; 2 g. saturated fat; 70 mg. cholesterol, 366 mg. sodium.

### SERVING SUGGESTIONS
Accompany with steamed green beans tossed with almond slivers.
   Also, serve orzo tossed with chopped parsley, lemon juice, olive oil, salt and pepper.

**SERVES 4**

# Spice-rubbed Glazed Pork Chops

romatic spices give these pork chops a distinctive flavor.

## You Will Need

½ teaspoon salt
¼ teaspoon cinnamon
¼ teaspoon allspice
4 lean bone-in pork chops, about 1½ pounds
1 tablespoon canola oil
¼ cup nonfat chicken broth
½ cup apple juice

**1.** Combine the salt, cinnamon and allspice in a small bowl. Sprinkle evenly over the pork chops.

**2.** Heat the oil in a nonstick skillet over medium high. Add the pork and cook for 4 minutes, or until the chops are browned and lift readily from the pan. Turn and cook for 3 to 4 more minutes.

**3.** Remove the pork from the pan and add the chicken broth and apple juice. Boil the liquid for about 6 minutes, or until it thickens into a syrup (when a spoon is drawn across it, it should take to the count of 3 for the line to disappear). Return the chops to the pan and turn to coat them with the glaze. Cook for 1 more minute, or until the chops are heated through. Top the chops with the glaze to serve.

### Nutritional Analysis

For each serving: 201 calories; 24 g. protein; 4 g. carbohydrates; 0 dietary fiber; 9 g. fat; 2.2 g. saturated fat; 70 mg. cholesterol, 405 mg. sodium.

### SERVING SUGGESTIONS

Serve with microwaved "baked" potatoes: Wash 4 evenly sized potatoes and pierce skin with fork in several places. Wrap each potato in a piece of paper towel and arrange in a spoke pattern on a microwave-proof plate. Microwave for 12 to 14 minutes, or until tender. (Take into account that they continue cooking after removed from microwave.) Cut the top open and fill each with 1 tablespoon light sour cream.

Also, serve steamed broccoli.

**SERVES 4**

# Fish & Shellfish

*Quick Shrimp Gumbo combines the classic elements of the famed stew.*

# Salmon Roasted with Tomato, Orange and Green Olives

What started out one day in my kitchen to be salmon Veracruz, the Mexican dish with tomato, chile, onion and lime, evolved into this dish. Perhaps it had to do with the ingredients I happened to lay my eyes upon, or that the night before I'd eaten a very different dish, which also combined the flavors of salmon and orange. Whichever, the result was this unusual, surprising and quite delicious dinner.

If you saute the vegetables in an oven-proof skillet, this can be made in one pot.

## You Will Need

1 tablespoon olive oil
1 onion, chopped
2 cloves garlic, minced
1 (14-ounce) can whole plum tomatoes in their juices
¼ teaspoon sugar
⅛ teaspoon red pepper flakes
¼ cup pimento-stuffed green olives, roughly chopped
2 tablespoons orange juice
1 teaspoon orange zest
1 ¼ pounds salmon fillet, cut in 4 pieces

**1.** Preheat the oven to 450 degrees.

**2.** Heat the oil in a nonstick skillet over medium high. Add the onion and garlic and cook, stirring occasionally, about 2 to 3 minutes, or until soft. Add the tomatoes, sugar, red pepper flakes, olives, orange juice and orange zest, and cook, breaking up the tomatoes with a spoon, for 5 minutes.

**3.** Place the salmon in a baking dish, top with the tomato mixture, and bake for 10 minutes, or until the salmon is still slightly translucent in the center of its thickest part. Serve immediately, topping the fish with the tomatoes and sauce.

**Nutritional Analysis**
For each serving: 308 calories; 29.8 g. protein; 9.6 g. carbohydrates; 2 g. dietary fiber; 16.5 g. fat; 3.24 g. saturated fat; 84 mg. cholesterol, 379 mg. sodium.

**SERVING SUGGESTIONS**
Accompany with almond rice: Cook white rice according to package instructions, substituting nonfat chicken broth for the water. Toss with slivered almonds and chopped cilantro to taste.

Also, steam broccoli, and serve it topped with a squirt of lemon juice and a small pat of butter.

# Pan-seared Salmon with Mustard Cilantro Topping

This recipe's method of searing lightly floured salmon will keep the fish moist, as long as you're careful about how long you leave the fish on the heat. The rule of thumb is 10 minutes per inch of thickness, but if you cook the fish slightly under that, by the time it reaches the table it will be done perfectly.

## You Will Need

¼ cup Dijon mustard
¼ cup light mayonnaise
¾ cup loosely packed
  cilantro leaves, chopped
¼ teaspoon salt
⅛ teaspoon pepper
2 tablespoons flour
1 ¼ pounds salmon fillet, cut in 4 pieces
1 tablespoon olive oil

**1.** Combine the mustard, mayonnaise and cilantro in a small bowl and set aside at room temperature.

**2.** Combine the salt, pepper and flour on a plate. Dredge the pieces of salmon in the mixture. Shake off any excess.

**3.** Heat the oil in a nonstick pan over medium high. Add the salmon and cook without moving for 5 to 6 minutes, or until browned. Turn the salmon and cook another 4 to 5 minutes, or until the fish is still slightly translucent in the center. Serve immediately, topping each piece of salmon with a dollop of the mustard sauce. Pass the extra sauce in a bowl.

### Nutritional Analysis
For each serving: 303 calories; 23 g. protein; 6 g. carbohydrates; <1 g. dietary fiber; 21 g. fat; 3.3 g. saturated fat; 67 mg. cholesterol, 696 mg. sodium.

### SERVING SUGGESTIONS
Accompany with steamed yellow and green summer squash cut into 2-inch-by-¼-inch sticks.
  Also, serve with a vegetable medley of lima beans, corn and peas tossed with a small pat of butter and salt to taste.

**SERVES 4**

# Salmon en Papillote

This elegant, light dinner is simple and tastes bright. Thankfully, it's low in calories, too. Cooking the fish in foil packets makes after-dinner cleanup a breeze.

## You Will Need

1 to 1 ¼ pounds salmon fillet, cut in 4 pieces
½ teaspoon salt
⅛ teaspoon pepper
2 scallions, chopped
1 tomato, cut in 1-inch pieces
½ teaspoon dried basil
2 tablespoons lemon juice
4 very thin slices lemon

**1.** Preheat the oven to 400 degrees.

**2.** Cut 4 (15-inch) lengths of foil. Fold each in half and then unfold to form a crease. Place a piece of salmon in the center of one side of each piece of foil. Sprinkle each piece of fish with the salt, pepper, scallions, tomato, basil and lemon juice, and top each with 1 slice of lemon.

**3.** Working with 1 foil package at a time, fold half the foil over the fillet. Roll the edges of the foil up and in, forming an enclosed package. Place the packets in the center of the oven for 8 to 10 minutes, depending on the thickness of the fillets (the rule is 10 minutes per inch of thickness), or until the packages are puffed. The salmon can be served in the packets, with a slit cut across the top to let the steam escape.

**Nutritional Analysis**
For each serving: 176 calories; 29 g. protein; 3 g. carbohydrates; 1 g. dietary fiber; 5 g. fat; <1 g. saturated fat; 74 mg. cholesterol, 390 mg. sodium.

**SERVING SUGGESTION**
Accompany with carrot-cumin soup: Saute ½ chopped onion and 1 teaspoon cumin in 1 ½ teaspoons olive oil. Add 1 pound thinly sliced carrots, 1 diced potato and 2 cups nonfat chicken broth and cook about 20 minutes, or until vegetables are very soft. Puree in batches in the bowl of a food processor (or in the pan using an immersion blender). Return the puree to the pan and add 1 to 2 cups fat-free milk until desired consistency is reached. Add salt and pepper to taste, and heat through.

**SERVES 4**

# Smothered Salmon

................................................................

Don't underestimate the wonderfully rich flavor you get by cooking this salmon under a thick layer of sauteed onions. It's important to cook the onions until tender before putting them on top of the fish to maximize their sweetness.

## You Will Need

1 tablespoon extra-virgin olive oil
2 onions, chopped (about 2 cups)
1 ½ teaspoons paprika
¼ teaspoon cayenne pepper
1 cup red wine
1 tablespoon tomato paste
1 teaspoon salt
1 ½ pounds salmon fillet
¼ cup water

**1.** Heat the oil over medium high in a large, 2-inch-deep pan with a lid. Add the onions and cook, stirring occasionally, for 3 minutes, or until softened. Stir in the paprika and cayenne and cook, stirring, 1 minute. Pour in the wine and tomato paste and cook for 4 minutes, or until the liquid becomes syrupy.

**2.** Sprinkle both sides of the salmon fillet with salt and add it to the pan (it may need to be cut in half to fit). Spoon as much of the onion and sauce as you can over the top of the fish and pour the water around the fillet.

**3.** Cover the pan, reduce the heat to medium, and cook for 12 to 15 minutes, or until the fish is still slightly translucent in the center. To serve, cut the fish into equal portions and spoon the sauce over the top.

### Nutritional Analysis
For each serving: 422 calories; 35 g. protein; 9 g. carbohydrates; 2 g. dietary fiber; 22 g. fat; 4.2 g. saturated fat; 100 mg. cholesterol, 720 mg. sodium.

### SERVING SUGGESTIONS
Accompany with a quick, warm potato salad: Quarter new potatoes and boil them in lightly salted water until they can be easily pierced with a fork. Drain, and while warm toss them with light mayonnaise and a pinch of rosemary.

Also, steam green beans until crisp-tender. Toss them with strips of prepared roasted red peppers, some of the liquid from the peppers and a splash of red wine vinegar.

**SERVES 4**

# Salmon Teriyaki

## Good Idea

**QUICK DESSERT:**
Tropical parfaits that combine coconut and mango sorbets make a refreshing dessert: Toast unsweetened coconut in a dry, hot skillet until lightly browned, and crumble some ginger-snap cookies. Layer the ingredients in glasses, starting with a scoop of slightly softened coconut sorbet. Top with crumbled gingersnaps, a scoop of mango sorbet and then another layer of ginger-snaps. Sprinkle with toasted coconut.

Once when we were visiting my mother, she mentioned that she had made fish for dinner. I quickly took my children aside and reminded them to smile and find something good to say about dinner, even if they didn't like it.

I was very proud of my son as he politely ate his dinner, and shocked when he asked for seconds. The teriyaki glaze gives the salmon an irresistible sweet sable-brown crust. Be sure to add the teriyaki sauce when the fish is just about cooked — it burns easily because of the honey.

## You Will Need

2 tablespoons low-sodium soy sauce
1 tablespoon honey
1 teaspoon minced fresh ginger
1 garlic clove, minced
1 tablespoon sesame oil
1 pound salmon fillet,
    cut in 4 pieces

**1.** Combine the soy sauce, honey, ginger and garlic in a small bowl, and stir until the honey is dissolved.

**2.** Heat the oil in a nonstick skillet over medium high. Add the fish, flesh side down, and cook without moving it for 3 to 4 minutes, or until golden brown. Turn the fish over and cook about 3 more minutes. Drizzle the sauce over the fillets, then turn them over so they are entirely coated in sauce. Continue cooking until the salmon is still slightly translucent in the center of the thickest part, about 1 to 2 minutes. Serve immediately, spooning the sauce from the pan over the fish.

### Nutritional Analysis
For each serving: 187 calories; 23 g. protein; 6 g. carbohydrates; <1 g. dietary fiber; 7.3 g. fat; 1.1 g. saturated fat; 59 mg. cholesterol, 329 mg. sodium.

### SERVING SUGGESTIONS
Accompany with sesame-scallion rice: Toss white rice with sesame seeds and thinly sliced scallions. Spoon any remaining sauce from the fish over the top.

Also, serve sugar snap peas or snow peas, cooked, if frozen, according to package instructions. If fresh, saute quickly over high heat until crisp-tender.

**SERVES 4**

# Lemon Pepper Salmon

Since fish is traditionally called brain food, I guess I can't call this dinner a no-brainer. But it's the sort of dish you make one time, and then dozens more without ever having to look at the recipe again.

The 1 tablespoon of butter gives the sauce richness and adds about 25 calories and 3 grams of fat to each serving. This recipe shows how butter, when used judiciously, adds a great deal to a healthful dish. In this case, the butter helps thicken the sauce as well as flavor the dish.

## You Will Need

1 ¼ pounds salmon fillet
1 teaspoon lemon pepper
1 teaspoon olive oil
2 tablespoons lemon juice
¼ cup white wine
1 tablespoon butter

**1.** Sprinkle the salmon with lemon pepper.

**2.** Heat the olive oil in a nonstick skillet over medium high. Add the salmon and cook about 4 to 5 minutes, or until golden. Turn the fish over and cook another 4 to 5 minutes, or until the salmon is still slightly translucent in the center. Remove the fish to a plate and cover with foil to keep it warm.

**3.** Turn the heat to high, and add the lemon juice and wine to the pan and cook 2 minutes. Add the butter and cook, stirring, until the sauce is thickened. Serve the fish and spoon sauce over the top.

### Nutritional Analysis
For each serving: 214 calories; 28 g. protein; 1 g. carbohydrates; <1 g. dietary fiber; 9 g. fat; 2.7 g. saturated fat; 82 mg. cholesterol, 194 mg. sodium.

### SERVING SUGGESTIONS
Accompany with steamed mixed vegetables: Steam together 1 carrot sliced thinly on the diagonal, small broccoli florets, and 1 small yellow squash cut in ¼-inch slices then in half. Toss with cherry or grape tomatoes that have been halved.

Also, serve with white rice tossed with dill, capers and chopped prepared roasted red peppers to taste.

**SERVES 4**

# Orange Teriyaki Swordfish Kebabs

I consider this a meat-eater's fish dinner. The texture of swordfish is meaty to begin with, and its flavor is decidedly un-fishy. Combine that with the fact that you're serving it kebab style — and with a slightly sweet sauce — and you may convert the non-fish eaters in the family.

## You Will Need

3 tablespoons low-sodium soy sauce
1 tablespoon rice vinegar
1 teaspoon fresh minced ginger
1 tablespoon honey
1 ½ pounds swordfish,
   cut in 1-inch pieces
10 ounces mushrooms, stems removed
1 green pepper, cut in 1 ½-inch pieces
1 red pepper, cut in 1 ½-inch pieces
6 tablespoons orange juice

**1.** Preheat the broiler. If using wooden skewers, soak them in water (to prevent them from burning) while you prepare the ingredients. Coat the broiler pan with cooking spray.

**2.** Combine the soy sauce, rice vinegar, ginger and honey in a bowl. Add the swordfish and toss to coat. Set aside for 15 minutes.

**3.** Thread the swordfish, mushrooms, green pepper and red pepper on 8 skewers, alternating ingredients. Broil the kebabs 5 minutes on each side, or until the fish is cooked through.

**4.** Meanwhile, pour the reserved marinade into a saucepan. Add the orange juice and bring to a boil over medium-high heat, and cook 10 minutes, or until slightly thick and syrupy. To serve, drizzle the sauce over the kebabs.

### Nutritional Analysis
For each serving: 277 calories; 37 g. protein; 16 g. carbohydrates; 2 g. dietary fiber; 7 g. fat; 2 g. saturated fat; 66 mg. cholesterol, 686 mg. sodium.

### SERVING SUGGESTIONS
Serve the kebabs over a bed of couscous cooked according to package directions, substituting nonfat chicken broth for water.

   Accompany with a shredded salad: Cut iceberg lettuce in long thin shreds. Shred carrots with a vegetable peeler. Combine them with thinly sliced red onion and green pepper and tomato cut into thin wedges. Toss with a light vinaigrette: 4 tablespoons extra-virgin olive oil, 2 tablespoons red wine vinegar, a generous pinch of sugar, ½ teaspoon dried or fresh dill, and salt and pepper to taste.

**SERVES 4**

# Panzanella with Tuna

Panzanella, the traditional bread and tomato salad, becomes a complete meal with the addition of canned tuna. It takes only a few minutes to prepare, but should sit for at least 10 minutes to allow the flavors to develop. It's the cook's prerogative to set a little aside for lunch the next day, when the flavors will have thoroughly saturated the bread.

## You Will Need

2 tablespoons red wine vinegar
½ cup extra-virgin olive oil
½ teaspoon salt
¼ teaspoon black pepper
¾ pound baguette (preferably stale), cut in ¾-inch cubes
1 ¾ pounds ripe tomatoes, cut in 1-inch pieces
1 red onion, chopped
1 cup fresh basil, chopped
¼ cup fresh mint, chopped
2 (6-ounce) cans tuna packed in water, drained

**1.** Combine the vinegar, oil, salt and pepper in a small bowl.

**2.** In a large bowl, toss together the bread cubes, tomatoes, onion, basil and mint. Pour the dressing over the bread and tomato mixture. Toss in tuna and let sit for at least 10 minutes before serving.

**Nutritional Analysis**
For each serving: 426 calories; 21 g. protein; 38 g. carbohydrates; 3.7 g. dietary fiber; 21 g. fat; 3.2 g. saturated fat; 17 mg. cholesterol, 744 mg. sodium.

**SERVING SUGGESTIONS**
Serve panzanella in individual bowls or on a bed of lettuce.

Accompany with green beans steamed until crisp-tender. The beans can be tossed right into the panzanella, if so desired.

**SERVES 6**

# Oven-roasted Vegetables with Halibut

## COOKING:

The general guideline for cooking fish is 10 minutes for every inch of thickness, but use your judgment, and check the fish a minute or two before that. Most fish should be cooked until it just turns opaque in the center — and remember it continues to cook after it is removed from the heat. Always check the thickest part of the fillet or the center of a steak.

Roasting vegetables gives them a taste and texture that can't be replicated by any other cooking method. It intensifies their inherent flavors and sugars. This recipe uses fast-roasting vegetables — tomatoes, bell peppers and onions. You can add any other vegetables you have on hand, but be sure to cut them to an appropriate size for the cooking time. I like to place the fish in the center of the pan with the vegetables around it, but you can also place the fish on top of the vegetables, which will cause the flavors to blend more.

## You Will Need

4 plum tomatoes,
    cut in quarters lengthwise
1 yellow bell pepper, cut in strips
1 green bell pepper, cut in strips
1 red onion, cut in ½-inch wedges
1 tablespoon extra-virgin olive oil
½ teaspoon salt, divided
⅛ teaspoon pepper
1 tablespoon Dijon mustard
2 teaspoons Worcestershire sauce
1 ¼ pounds halibut, about 1 inch thick,
    cut in 4 pieces

**1.** Preheat the oven to 500 degrees.

**2.** In a large baking dish, toss together the tomatoes, yellow and green peppers, onion, oil, ¼ teaspoon of the salt and pepper. Roast the vegetables for 15 minutes, stirring occasionally.

**3.** Combine the mustard, Worcestershire and remaining ¼ teaspoon of salt and spread the mixture over the fish. Add the fish to the vegetables and roast about 10 minutes, or until the fish is opaque and cooked through. Serve the fish with vegetables on the side.

### Nutritional Analysis
For each serving: 238 calories; 31.3 g. protein; 11 g. carbohydrates; 2.5 g. dietary fiber; 7.5 g. fat; 1.4 g. saturated fat; 45 mg. cholesterol, 498 mg. sodium.

### SERVING SUGGESTION
Accompany with microwaved "baked" potatoes: Pierce 4 potatoes all over with a fork and wrap individually in paper towels. Arrange them in a spoke pattern in the microwave and cook on high for 12 to 14 minutes, turning once halfway through cooking (cooking times will vary according to the size of the potatoes and individual microwave ovens). Potatoes are done when they are easily pierced with a fork. To serve, split them open, fill with a mixture of light sour cream and fresh cut chives.

**SERVES 4**

# Pan-seared Halibut Steaks with Plum Salsa

·················································································································································

This salsa takes only a few minutes to assemble. Make it first so the flavors can develop while you cook the fish. The salsa will keep several days in the refrigerator, and makes an excellent accompaniment to grilled or broiled pork.

## You Will Need

**FOR THE SALSA:**
¾ cup loosely packed cilantro leaves
¼ cup loosely packed mint leaves
1 pound plums, roughly chopped
½ red onion, cut into chunks
1 tablespoon apple cider vinegar
3 tablespoons orange juice
¼ teaspoon red pepper flakes
½ teaspoon salt

**FOR THE HALIBUT:**
2 teaspoons olive oil
4 (6-ounce) halibut steaks,
  about 1 inch thick

**1.** To make the salsa, combine the cilantro and mint in the bowl of a food processor and pulse several times until they are chopped, stopping to scrape down sides. Add the plums and onion, and pulse until they are chopped in ¼-inch pieces. Transfer to a bowl, and stir in the vinegar, orange juice, red pepper flakes and salt. Set aside, loosely covered, at room temperature.

**2.** To pan-sear the halibut, heat the oil over medium high in a nonstick skillet large enough to hold the fish in a single layer without crowding. Add the halibut and cook for 5 minutes, turn, and cook another 5 minutes. Fish will be lightly browned on both sides. Remove the fish from the pan and serve immediately, topped with the plum salsa.

**Nutritional Analysis**
For each serving: 282 calories; 37 g. protein; 18 g. carbohydrates; 2.2 g. dietary fiber; 6.9 g. fat; 1.4 g. saturated fat; 54 mg. cholesterol, 385 mg. sodium.

**SERVING SUGGESTION**
Accompany with zucchini fingers: Cut 2 medium zucchini into fourths lengthwise, then across in 2-inch pieces. Dip in lightly beaten egg (or egg white), then in a mixture of equal parts cornmeal and flour. Saute in canola oil, about 6 to 8 minutes or until tender and golden.

**SERVES 4**

# Caribbean Halibut with Mango Basil Sauce

This halibut has the appeal of fried fish. The preparation gives it a golden-brown crust that is not only delicious but seals in the moisture. The fat-free sauce is sweet and spicy, and is as delicious over plain rice as it is over fish, chicken or pork.

To make preparation as simple as can be, buy a large, 1-inch-thick halibut steak and cut it in half on either side of the bone. Then remove the skin and cut the flesh into chunks.

## You Will Need

**FOR THE SAUCE:**
1 mango, peeled
1 cup nonfat chicken broth
1 ½ tablespoons brown sugar
2 tablespoons low-sodium soy sauce
⅛ teaspoon cayenne pepper, or to taste
½ cup basil leaves, chopped

**FOR THE FISH:**
1 ¼ pounds halibut,
   cut into 1-inch chunks
2 tablespoons flour
½ teaspoon salt
2 tablespoons canola oil
1 red pepper, cut into 1-inch pieces

**1.** To make the sauce, puree the mango in the bowl of a food processor. Combine the mango, chicken broth, sugar, soy sauce and cayenne in a small saucepan, bring to a boil, reduce the heat and simmer 8 to 10 minutes, or until the sauce has thickened some. Remove the mixture from the heat and stir in the basil.

**2.** To make the fish, combine the halibut, flour and salt in a bowl. Heat the oil over medium high in a large skillet, add halibut, and cook without touching it for 3 minutes, or until golden brown. Turn the pieces of fish, add the red pepper to the skillet and cook 3 more minutes, or until the underside of the fish is browned and the peppers are crisp-tender. To serve, spoon warmed sauce over fish and peppers.

### Nutritional Analysis
For each serving: 302 calories; 32 g. protein; 20 g. carbohydrates; 1.7 g. dietary fiber; 10.3 g. fat; 1 g. saturated fat; 45 mg. cholesterol, 784 mg. sodium.

### SERVING SUGGESTIONS
Serve the fish over a bed of white rice and top with extra sauce.

Also, serve with a plain steamed vegetable, such as broccoli or green beans.

**SERVES 4**

# Vegetable-steamed Snapper

Cooking fish in a skillet on a bed of lightly sauteed vegetables and a small amount of liquid keeps it juicy. You're essentially using the vegetables as your steaming rack.

## You Will Need

1 tablespoon extra-virgin olive oil
1 onion, diced
2 garlic cloves, minced
1 green pepper, diced
1 teaspoon dried thyme
1 tomato (about ½ pound), diced
2 tablespoons lime juice
¼ cup water
½ teaspoon salt
1 ¼ pounds red snapper fillets
½ teaspoon grated lime zest

**1.** Heat the oil in a skillet large enough to hold the fish in a single layer. Add the onion, garlic, green pepper and thyme, and cook, stirring, 5 minutes or until vegetables are very soft.

**2.** Add the tomato, lime juice and water, turn the heat to simmer and place the fish over the vegetables. Sprinkle the top of the fish with salt, then spoon a small amount of the vegetables and their liquid over the top of the fish. Cover the pan and simmer 10 minutes. Serve the fish with the vegetable mixture spooned over the top and sprinkle with the zest.

**Nutritional Analysis**
For each serving: 213 calories; 30 g. protein; 9 g. carbohydrates; 2 g. dietary fiber; 6 g. fat; <1 g. saturated fat; 52 mg. cholesterol, 389 mg. sodium.

**SERVING SUGGESTION**
Serve with parsley potatoes: Cut 1 pound new potatoes in quarters; place in a saucepan with enough cold water to cover. Bring to a boil and simmer until tender, about 25 minutes. Toss with 1 tablespoon olive oil, chopped parsley and salt and pepper.

**SERVES 4**

# Roasted Flounder

It wasn't all that long ago that fat phobia was at its peak and many of us eschewed recipes calling for butter and/or cream. I still try to cook with a minimum of saturated fat, but have learned through trial and error that a small amount goes a long way. This recipe is a perfect example: A mere 1 ½ tablespoons of butter results in a silky, rich sauce and gives full flavor to every bite.

The pendulum has swung back and forth between the health benefits and dangers of butter and margarine too many times to count. I resolve it in my mind quite simply: A little butter adds far more to most dishes than does a lot of margarine.

## You Will Need

1 ½ pounds flounder
2 tablespoons lemon juice
1 teaspoon lemon zest
⅓ cup white wine
1 tablespoon capers
½ teaspoon fennel seeds
1 ½ tablespoons butter, cut in small bits

**1.** Preheat the oven to 500 degrees.

**2.** Place the flounder in a single layer in a baking dish. Sprinkle with lemon juice, zest, wine, capers and fennel seeds. Top with bits of butter.

**3.** Roast in the oven about 13 to 15 minutes, or until the fish just loses its translucency in the thickest part of the center. Remove from oven and cut in 4 even pieces. Stir the sauce remaining in pan and spoon over fish.

**Nutritional Analysis**
For each serving: 209 calories; 32 g. protein; <1 g. carbohydrates; 0 dietary fiber; 6 g. fat; 3 g. saturated fat; 93 mg. cholesterol, 262 mg. sodium.

**SERVING SUGGESTIONS**
Serve with braised fennel: Heat 2 tablespoons extra-virgin olive oil in a large skillet. Add 1 thinly sliced fennel bulb and cook over medium high for about 2 minutes. Add ½ cup of nonfat chicken broth, salt and pepper, and cook about 15 minutes, or until fennel is tender and there is little or no liquid left in the pan.

Accompany with steamed broccoli and rice tossed with canned diced Italian-seasoned tomatoes.

**SERVES 4**

# Tilapia with Pesto

......................................................................................................................................

Every now and then I come up with a dish that is so embarrassingly obvious that it doesn't even seem to warrant a recipe. This is one of them. I like tilapia, sometimes called St. Peter's fish, but any mild-flavored white fish can be used. However, I've found that you can't use the 10-minute-an-inch cooking rule when you make tilapia this way. When using 1-inch-thick fillets, cook for 20 minutes — the tomatoes keep the tilapia moist.

## You Will Need

1 (14 ½-ounce) can diced tomatoes
2 teaspoons balsamic vinegar
1 ¼ pounds tilapia, or
   a mild white fish, such as flounder
1 tablespoon prepared bottled pesto

**1.** Preheat the oven to 400 degrees.

**2.** Pour the tomatoes in the bottom of a baking dish (large enough to hold the fish fillets in a single layer). Stir in the vinegar. Lay the fillets on top of the tomatoes in a single layer, and spread a thin layer of pesto over them. Cover the dish loosely with foil and bake for 20 minutes (if using 1-inch-thick tilapia), or until the center of the fish is just opaque.

### Nutritional Analysis
For each serving: 167 calories; 30 g. protein; 1.5 g. carbohydrates; <1 g. dietary fiber; 3.7 g. fat; <1 g. saturated fat; 76 mg. cholesterol, 175 mg. sodium.

### SERVING SUGGESTIONS
Serve fish on a bed of white rice and spoon extra tomatoes over the top.
   Accompany with sauteed chick-pea and watercress salad: Saute minced garlic and drained and rinsed chick-peas in olive oil. Toss with watercress, a healthy splash of balsamic vinegar, a splash of olive oil, and salt and pepper to taste.

**SERVES 4**

# Cod in a Sea of Vegetables

## Good Idea

**QUICK START:**
Serve Middle Eastern-flavored hummus with pita bread, crackers or raw vegetables. A simple version is made by combining drained and rinsed chickpeas, minced garlic and sesame tahini (peanut butter may be substituted in a pinch) in the bowl of a food processor and pulsing until the mixture is fairly smooth. Scrap down the sides, and with the motor running, add in extra-virgin olive oil until desired consistency is reached. Add salt and pepper to taste.

Cod was the fish we ate most often when I was growing up, but it seemed to fall out of favor with cooks in the last 10 years or so. Now it's starting to reappear on restaurant menus as well as dinner tables, and with good reason — it's mild and sweet, and holds up well to a variety of cooking techniques.

### You Will Need

1 tablespoon olive oil
1 onion, chopped
3 cloves garlic, minced
1 green pepper, sliced
1 yellow squash (about ½ pound),
   cut in half lengthwise, then sliced
½ teaspoon cumin
½ teaspoon salt
¼ teaspoon pepper
¼ teaspoon Tabasco
1 (14 ½-ounce) can diced tomatoes
1 to 1 ½ pounds cod
   (or similar white fish)

**1.** Heat the oil in a 2-inch-deep skillet or in a Dutch oven over medium high. Add the onion, garlic and green pepper, and cook, stirring 2 to 3 minutes, or until softened. Add the yellow squash and cook another 2 minutes.

**2.** Stir in the cumin, salt, pepper, Tabasco and tomatoes, and bring the mixture to a boil. Immediately reduce the heat so the mixture simmers.

**3.** Lay the fish over the vegetables in a single layer. Spoon a little of the liquid (not the vegetables) over the fish. Cover the pan and simmer for about 7 minutes, depending on the thickness of the fish. When the fish turns opaque, remove the pan from the heat (the fish will continue cooking for at least 2 minutes). To serve, place fillets on plates and top with vegetables and juice.

**Nutritional Analysis**
For each serving: 205 calories; 27.6 g. protein; 13 g. carbohydrates; 3.3 g. dietary fiber; 4.7 g. fat; <1 g. saturated fat; 61 mg. cholesterol, 252 mg. sodium.

**SERVING SUGGESTION**
Accompany with microwaved "baked" potatoes: Pierce 4 potatoes all over with a fork and wrap individually in paper towels. Arrange them in a spoke pattern in the microwave and cook on high for 12 to 14 minutes, turning once halfway through cooking (cooking time will vary according to the size of the potatoes and individual microwave ovens). Potatoes are done when they are easily pierced with a fork. To serve, split them open, fill with a mixture of light sour cream and fresh cut chives.

**SERVES 4**

# Spanish Catfish

Though you might not normally think of combining spices such as cinnamon and cloves with fish, it works quite well. The key is to keep the strong flavors in balance — too much overwhelms the fish.

## You Will Need

1 tablespoon extra-virgin olive oil
3 cloves garlic, minced
1 jalapeno pepper, seeded and
  minced (or more to taste)
¼ cup cilantro, chopped
½ teaspoon cinnamon
Pinch of ground cloves
½ teaspoon cumin
½ teaspoon salt
1 ¼ pounds plum tomatoes, chopped
½ cup white wine
1 ¼ pounds catfish fillets

**1.** Heat the oil over medium high in a deep skillet that has a lid. Add the garlic and jalapeno, and cook, stirring, for 3 minutes.

**2.** Add the cilantro, cinnamon, cloves, cumin and salt, and stir. Add the tomatoes and wine, and cook 2 minutes.

**3.** Lay the fish over the tomato mixture in a single layer. Spoon some of the mixture over the fish, cover, and reduce the heat to low. Cook for 15 minutes, or until the fish is cooked through. Serve the fish with the tomato sauce.

### Nutritional Analysis
For each serving: 224 calories; 23 g. protein; 3 g. carbohydrates; <1 g. dietary fiber; 11 g. fat; 2.5 g. saturated fat; 67 mg. cholesterol, 372 mg. sodium.

### SERVING SUGGESTIONS
Serve the fish over a bed of white rice.
   Accompany with wilted spinach: Place cleaned, fresh spinach in a hot pan with only the water from rinsing clinging to its leaves. Toss the spinach as it cooks, and remove the pan from the heat as soon as the leaves are wilted. Add a small pat of butter and a pinch of nutmeg to the pan and toss. Season with salt and pepper to taste.

**SERVES 4**

# Cornmeal-crusted Catfish with Mustard Sauce

This fish develops a beautiful golden crust that sets it apart from standard fare. The trick to keeping the crust intact when you turn the fish is to make sure that it is cooked over high heat; the cornmeal will remain soggy if your heat is too low.

## You Will Need

⅓ cup yellow cornmeal
2 tablespoons flour
½ teaspoon dried thyme
1 large egg
¼ cup spicy brown mustard
½ cup milk, divided
1 pound catfish fillets, cut into 4 pieces
1 tablespoon canola oil
Tabasco to taste

**1.** Combine the cornmeal, flour and thyme in a bowl and set aside. In another bowl, lightly beat the egg, add the mustard and ¼ cup of the milk and stir to combine.

**2.** Dip the fish in the egg mixture. Then dredge the fish in the cornmeal mixture, thoroughly coating it. Set the fillets on a clean plate as you work.

**3.** Heat the oil in a large, nonstick pan over medium high. Add the fish in a single layer. When the fish is lightly browned and no longer sticks (gently test by turning one piece), about 3 minutes, turn it over to brown the second side. After about 2 minutes, reduce heat to medium and cook another 5 to 6 minutes, or until the thickest part of the fish is opaque inside. Remove fish from pan and cover it with foil to keep it warm.

**4.** Add the remaining egg mixture to the skillet and slowly stir in the remaining ¼ cup of milk. Cook, stirring, over medium heat for about 2 minutes. Add Tabasco to taste. Divide fish among serving plates and spoon the mustard sauce over the pieces.

**Nutritional Analysis**
For each serving: 287 calories; 23 g. protein; 14 g. carbohydrates; 1.4 g dietary fiber; 15 g. fat; 3.2 g. saturated fat; 108 mg. cholesterol, 288 mg. sodium.

**SERVING SUGGESTIONS**
Accompany with tomato rice: Cook 1 cup white rice according to package directions, adding 1 bay leaf to the cooking water. Toss cooked rice with 2 chopped plum tomatoes, chopped fresh parsley to taste, and salt and pepper to taste.
Also, serve steamed broccoli.

**SERVES 4**

# Catfish Baked with Winter Salsa

People tend to want to fry catfish, a technique that was ideal for the stronger-flavored fish that was available before catfish was farmed. Farmed catfish is certainly delicious when fried, but it is equally well suited to baking (a far less messy and lower-fat way to cook).

The winter salsa features vegetables that are available all year round. Adding a few dashes of Tabasco will give the dish just a suggestion of heat.

## You Will Need

1¼ pounds catfish
½ teaspoon salt
¼ teaspoon pepper
1 pound (7 to 8) plum tomatoes
1 cup loosely packed parsley, chopped
1 large green pepper, diced
1 yellow pepper, diced
1 tablespoon lemon juice
Tabasco (optional)

**1.** Preheat the oven to 375 degrees. Sprinkle the catfish with the salt and pepper and place it in a 9-by-13-inch baking dish.

**2.** Cut the tomatoes in half and squeeze out the seeds as you would squeeze a lemon. Dice the flesh and combine it with the parsley, green and yellow peppers, lemon juice and a few dashes of Tabasco (if using). Pour the mixture over the fish. Bake for 25 to 30 minutes, basting the fish with the liquid from the bottom of the pan once or twice during cooking. Serve immediately.

**Nutritional Analysis**
For each serving: 243 calories; 24 g. protein; 12 g. carbohydrates; 3 g. dietary fiber; 11 g. fat; 3 g. saturated fat; 67 mg. cholesterol, 384 mg. sodium.

**SERVING SUGGESTIONS**
Serve with curried white rice pilaf: Heat 1 tablespoon olive oil in a saucepan. Add 1 to 2 teaspoons curry powder and cook, stirring, for 30 seconds. Add 1 cup converted rice and stir to coat. Add 2 cups chicken broth, bring to a boil, reduce heat and cover. Cook for 20 minutes, then let stand for 5 minutes.

Also, serve with wilted spinach: In a large skillet, heat a small amount of olive oil and minced garlic over medium-high heat, about 1 minute. Place cleaned, fresh spinach in the pan with only the water from rinsing clinging to its leaves. Toss the spinach as it cooks and remove the pan from the heat as soon as the leaves are wilted. Season with salt and pepper to taste.

**SERVES 4**

# Catfish Baked with Mustard and Capers

Baking this catfish in liquid in a covered dish essentially steams it. The result is moist and tender fish infused with the flavors of the other ingredients. And because you simply stick it in the oven, it is even more hassle-free than a quick saute. I like to use the free time to make a special side dish, or help with my kids' homework.

## You Will Need

1 ¼ pounds catfish fillets
1 tablespoon Dijon mustard
1 pound tomatoes, chopped
    into 1-inch pieces
1 tablespoon capers
¼ cup water

**1.** Preheat the oven to 375 degrees. Lay the catfish fillets in a single layer in a baking dish. Spread a thin coating of mustard on top of the fish.

**2.** Combine the tomatoes, capers and water in a bowl and pour over the top of the fish. Cover the baking dish with foil and bake for 15 minutes. Remove the foil and bake another 10 minutes. Serve immediately.

### Nutritional Analysis
For each serving: 164 calories; 25 g. protein; 6 g. carbohydrates; 1.5 g. dietary fiber; 4.8 g. fat; 1 g. saturated fat; 82 mg. cholesterol, 245 mg. sodium.

### SERVING SUGGESTIONS
Accompany with pignoli nut-parsley rice: Toss white rice with ½ cup pignoli (pine) nuts, ½ cup chopped fresh parsley, and salt and pepper to taste.

   Also, serve a quick summer squash saute: Cut yellow squash and zucchini lengthwise into eighths lengthwise, then across in 2-inch sticks and toss with salt and pepper. Heat 1 tablespoon of olive oil in a nonstick skillet over medium high. Add squash in a single layer and let it cook (without stirring) until lightly brown. Turn and cook again until brown and fork tender. Sprinkle with a dash of dried thyme and serve immediately.

**SERVES 4**

# Fisherman's Stew

This dish is inspired by the wonderful stews of Portugal. This short-cut method uses precooked mussels in brine (sold in jars) and canned clams. It can also be made with clams and mussels in the shell, in which case, you'll have to allow a little more time for cleaning the shellfish. This stew calls for saffron, an expensive spice that is often kept behind the store counters because it is sold in tiny quantities. Splurge on the real thing, though — it takes only a pinch to give color and distinctive flavor to dishes, and it keeps well.

## You Will Need

Pinch of saffron (about ⅛ teaspoon)
2 tablespoons hot water
1 tablespoon olive oil
1 onion, chopped
3 cloves garlic, minced
2 (8-ounce) bottles clam juice
1 (14 ½-ounce) can nonfat chicken broth
1 (15-ounce can) whole plum tomatoes, chopped in their juices
½ teaspoon oregano
1 to 1 ¼ pounds cod fillet, cut in 1-inch chunks
1 (10-ounce) can whole small clams, drained
1 (12-ounce) jar mussels in brine, drained

**1.** Combine the saffron and hot water in a small bowl and set aside for 10 minutes.

**2.** Heat the oil in a large Dutch oven over medium high. Add the onion and garlic, and cook 2 minutes. Add the clam juice, chicken broth, tomatoes, oregano and saffron water, and bring to a boil. Reduce heat and simmer 5 minutes.

**3.** Add the cod, and cook 3 minutes. Add the clams and mussels, and simmer 2 minutes. Serve immediately.

### Nutritional Analysis
For each serving: 225 calories; 36 g. protein; 9 g. carbohydrates; 1.2 g. dietary fiber; 5.3 g. fat; <1 g. saturated fat; 106 mg. cholesterol, 1203 mg. sodium.

### SERVING SUGGESTIONS
Accompany with garlic bread: Cut a baguette into ½-inch-thick slices. Brush the slices with olive oil. Toast them until they are golden, then rub with a cut garlic clove.

Also, serve a mixed greens salad with a creamy buttermilk mustard vinaigrette: 1 tablespoon vinegar, ½ teaspoon Dijon mustard, 1 tablespoon extra-virgin olive oil, ¼ cup low-fat buttermilk, ½ teaspoon sugar and pepper to taste.

**SERVES 6**

# Shrimp with Lime and Cilantro

This is a dish with simple clean flavors in just the right combination. And you can have it on the table in 15 to 20 minutes.

## You Will Need

1 pound shrimp, peeled
1 tablespoon plus 2 teaspoons lime juice
½ teaspoon cumin
1 tablespoon olive oil
2 cloves garlic, minced
½ teaspoon salt
¼ teaspoon pepper
1 cup fresh cilantro, chopped
1 teaspoon lime zest

**1.** Toss the shrimp with the lime juice and cumin. Heat the oil in a 10-inch skillet, add the garlic and the shrimp, and cook 4 to 5 minutes, stirring occasionally, or until the shrimp are just pink. Stir in the salt, pepper, cilantro and lime zest, and serve immediately.

### Nutritional Analysis

For each serving: 154 calories; 23 g. protein; 2.2 g. carbohydrates; <1 g. dietary fiber; 5.4 g. fat; <1 g. saturated fat; 172 mg. cholesterol, 460 mg. sodium.

### SERVING SUGGESTIONS

Serve shrimp over Mexican rice: Add ⅓ cup salsa, or more if desired, to cooked white rice.

Also accompany with a side dish that combines 1 (10-ounce) package of frozen chopped spinach, cooked according to package instructions, and 1 cup cooked corn. Toss with olive oil, a dash of nutmeg, and salt and pepper to taste.

**SERVES 4**

# Glazed Shrimp and Green Beans

This Chinese-style shrimp dish is sweet and savory — and on the table in about 20 minutes, including the time it takes to peel the shrimp. It's also extremely low in calories and fat. By tossing the shrimp with sherry and cornstarch, you'll slightly change the texture of the shrimp; it gets a somewhat silken exterior and the sauce clings to it better.

## You Will Need

1 tablespoon sherry
1 tablespoon plus 1 teaspoon cornstarch, divided
1 pound shrimp, peeled
1 teaspoon Worcestershire sauce
1 tablespoon tomato paste
1 tablespoon hoisin sauce
½ cup water
2 teaspoons sesame oil
2 cloves garlic, minced
1 tablespoon minced ginger
1 pound green beans,
    cut into 1-inch pieces

**1.** Combine the sherry and 1 tablespoon cornstarch in a bowl. Toss with the shrimp and set aside.

**2.** Dissolve the remaining 1 teaspoon of cornstarch in the Worcestershire. Add the tomato paste, hoisin and water.

**3.** Heat the sesame oil in a wok or large skillet. Add the garlic and ginger, and stir-fry 15 seconds. Add the green beans and stir-fry 15 seconds. Add the shrimp mixture and stir-fry 30 seconds. Add the sauce and cook about 4 minutes, stirring occasionally, or until the shrimp turn pink and the green beans are crisp-tender.

### Nutritional Analysis

For each serving: 205 calories; 26 g. protein; 15 g. carbohydrates; 4.2 g. dietary fiber; 4.5 g fat; <1 g. saturated fat; 173 mg. cholesterol, 286 mg. sodium.

### SERVING SUGGESTION

Accompany with white basmati rice tossed with chopped fresh cilantro to taste.

**Good Idea**

**SHOPPING:**
Don't dismiss frozen, uncooked shrimp. It tastes as good as "fresh" (which has usually been frozen for shipping and then thawed) and, because it can be kept on hand, it's more convenient. It's usually less expensive than the fresh, and sometimes it can be bought already deveined. To use, let it thaw in a bowl of cold water for about 10 minutes, then peel.

# Shrimp and Vegetables in Mediterranean Rice

This dish has the flavors of a paella and the creamy consistency of a risotto. The recipe doesn't specify that the shrimp must be peeled — that's the cook's choice. The paella will have wonderful flavor either way, and it saves you a few minutes in preparation if you serve the shrimp in the shell and let diners peel as they eat.

## You Will Need

¼ cup hot water
⅛ teaspoon saffron
2 tablespoons olive oil
1 onion, chopped
2 cloves garlic, minced
1 green pepper, diced
1½ cups short-grain white rice
1 package frozen artichoke hearts, thawed
1 (14½-ounce) can diced tomatoes
3 cups nonfat chicken broth
½ teaspoon salt
1 pound shrimp
1 (7-ounce) jar roasted red peppers, diced
1 cup frozen peas

**1.** Combine the hot water and saffron in a small bowl and set aside.

**2.** In a large skillet, heat the oil over medium high. Add the onion, garlic and green pepper and cook, stirring, for 3 minutes or until soft. Add the rice and stir thoroughly to coat. Add the artichokes, tomatoes and chicken broth, and bring to a boil.

**3.** Add the saffron water and salt. Cover and cook over medium for 15 minutes. Stir in the shrimp, roasted peppers and peas, and cook for 5 minutes, or until the liquid is absorbed, the rice is tender and the shrimp are cooked through. Serve in bowls.

**Nutritional Analysis**
For each serving: 483 calories; 33 g. protein; 70 g. carbohydrates; 6.7 g. dietary fiber; 9.6 g. fat; 1.5 g. saturated fat; 172 mg. cholesterol, 1315 g. sodium.

**SERVING SUGGESTION**
This dish is set off nicely by a first-course of melon wedges draped or wrapped with thinly sliced ham, preferably prosciutto.

**SERVES 4**

# Quick Shrimp Gumbo

There's something festive about making a big pot of gumbo — even when you're throwing it together quickly on a busy weeknight. In keeping with this dinner's theme, I like to doctor up a box of corn-muffin mix and bake the muffins in mini tins (they cook faster that way and somehow seem more fun to eat). Start the muffins before the gumbo to ensure they're done on time. And don't let the shrimp sit in the pot too long, or they overcook and get tough.

## You Will Need

1 teaspoon plus 1 tablespoon canola oil, divided
6 ounces precooked chicken or turkey sausage (preferably spicy), sliced
1 onion, chopped
2 celery stalks, sliced
2 cloves garlic, minced
1 green pepper, diced
2 tablespoons flour
1 (10-ounce) box frozen okra, slightly thawed
1 (14½-ounce) can nonfat chicken broth
Tabasco to taste (start with 2 dashes)
½ teaspoon thyme
½ teaspoon oregano
1 bay leaf
½ cup crushed canned tomatoes
1 pound shrimp, peeled

**1.** Heat 1 teaspoon of oil over medium in a large, 2-inch-deep skillet. Add the sausage, onion, celery, garlic and green pepper, and cook about 4 minutes, or until vegetables are soft.

**2.** Using a slotted spoon, remove the ingredients from the skillet. Add the remaining 1 tablespoon of oil, sprinkle with the flour, and cook, stirring constantly, until the flour browns. Return the sausage mixture to the pan and add the okra, chicken broth, Tabasco, thyme, oregano, bay leaf and tomatoes. Simmer for 15 minutes.

**3.** Add the shrimp and cook 5 more minutes, or until the shrimp are pink and just cooked through. Taste and add more hot sauce as desired. Serve in bowls.

### Nutritional Analysis

For each serving: 308 calories; 33 g. protein; 17 g. carbohydrates; 5 g. dietary fiber; 12.3 g. fat; 2.3 g. saturated fat; 210 mg. cholesterol, 923 mg. sodium.

### SERVING SUGGESTIONS

Serve the gumbo over a bed of white rice.

Accompany with "jazzy" corn muffins: Use a store-bought mix for cornbread or corn muffins and mix according to package instructions. Add minced jalapeno or canned diced green chiles to taste and ¼ cup light Cheddar cheese, and mix lightly. Bake according to package instructions.

Also, serve a crunchy salad made of Romaine lettuce, radishes, cucumber, celery and shredded carrots. Toss with a creamy buttermilk mustard vinaigrette: 1 tablespoon vinegar, ½ teaspoon Dijon mustard, 1 tablespoon extra-virgin olive oil, ¼ cup low-fat buttermilk, ½ teaspoon sugar and pepper to taste.

**Good Idea**

**COOKING:**
Keep a resealable bag in your freezer for uncooked shrimp shells, and add to it every time you serve shrimp. The shells can be used to infuse broth with a pure seafood flavor before using to make fish stews and gumbo.

# Sauteed Shrimp with Garlic, Lemon and Parsley

## COOKING:

One great time-saving gadget is the zester, a small tool with a series of holes at one end that makes pulling the zest off citrus a snap. You can also use a grater, but a zester is easier to use and clean. If a recipe calls for both zest and juice, zest before juicing. Also, you can freeze left-over zest in resealable bags, in teaspoon portions, for instance, that can be added instantly to sauces, vegetables and rice without measuring.

This classic flavor combination endures because it's so delicious — and cooks love the ease with which this dish can be thrown together.

## You Will Need

1 pound shrimp, peeled
½ teaspoon salt
¼ teaspoon pepper
1 tablespoon olive oil
3 cloves garlic, minced
2 tablespoons lemon juice
1 teaspoon lemon zest
1 cup fresh parsley, finely chopped

**1.** Toss the shrimp with the salt and pepper. Heat the oil over medium-high heat, add the garlic, and cook for 15 seconds, stirring. Add the shrimp and cook for 4 to 5 minutes, stirring occasionally, until the shrimp are lightly browned. Remove from heat and stir in the lemon juice, lemon zest and parsley. Serve immediately.

**Nutritional Analysis**
For each serving: 160 calories; 24 g. protein; 3.6 g. carbohydrates; <1 g. dietary fiber; 5.4 g. fat; <1 g. saturated fat; 172 mg. cholesterol, 465 mg. sodium.

**SERVING SUGGESTIONS**
To serve, mound the shrimp on a bed of cooked linguine that has been moistened with nonfat chicken broth and clam juice and tossed with olive oil, salt and pepper.

Accompany with tomato and cucumber salad: Thinly slice and salt tomatoes, a red onion, and a cucumber and drain in a colander for 15 minutes. Toss with an Italian vinaigrette made of 1 tablespoon red wine vinegar, 2 tablespoons extra-virgin olive oil, a dash of dried oregano and ½ teaspoon sugar.

**SERVES 4**

# Balsamic Glazed Scallops on Rice

Because scallops cook so quickly — in less than five minutes — they make an ideal weeknight meal. Be sure not to overcook them, because they easily become tough and chewy. You can use either the large sea scallops or the smaller bay scallops, but adjust your cooking time so that they cook until they just turn opaque; they will continue to cook after they are removed from the pan.

## You Will Need

**FOR THE RICE:**
2 cups water
1 tablespoon balsamic vinegar
¼ teaspoon salt
1 cup long-grain rice

**FOR THE SCALLOPS:**
3 tablespoons balsamic vinegar
¼ teaspoon salt
1 tablespoon plus 2 teaspoons honey
¼ teaspoon marjoram
1 tablespoon olive oil
1 pound scallops

**1.** To make the rice, bring the water, vinegar and salt to a boil, add rice, reduce the heat to low, cover and cook 20 minutes. Remove from heat and let stand, covered, 5 minutes.

**2.** Combine the balsamic vinegar, salt, honey, marjoram and olive oil in a large, nonstick skillet. Cook about 45 seconds over medium-high heat, or until the mixture starts to sizzle and boil. Add the scallops in a single layer and cook 3 minutes, stirring occasionally. Remove the scallops from the pan with a slotted spoon, and bring the remaining liquid to a boil. Boil 2 to 3 minutes, or until the mixture becomes syrupy. Return the scallops to the pan just to toss with the glaze. Immediately serve the scallops, placing them on a bed of the prepared rice, topping with extra sauce.

**Nutritional Analysis**
For each serving: 335 calories; 22 g. protein; 49 g. carbohydrates; <1g. dietary fiber; 4.6 g. fat; <1g. saturated fat; 37 mg. cholesterol, 480 mg. sodium.

**SERVING SUGGESTION**
Serve with steamed broccoli florets drizzled with a light Dijon vinaigrette: 1 to 2 tablespoons balsamic vinegar, 3 tablespoons extra-virgin olive oil, ½ teaspoon Dijon mustard or to taste, and salt and pepper to taste.

**SERVES 4**

# Pasta

*A creamy, yet light sauce envelops Penne and Vegetables with Chick-pea Vinaigrette.*

# Rotini with Chick-peas, Spinach and Fontina

This vegetarian pasta dinner has all the right stuff: nutrients galore, a healthful level of fat and, most importantly, creamy, delicious flavor. From start to finish, this dinner should take about 20 minutes to make. Although this makes a complete, well-balanced meal, a salad rounds it out nicely, and offers some crunchy contrast. You can omit the red pepper flakes from the recipe and let diners add them according to individual taste at the table.

## You Will Need

12 ounces rotini
2 (10-ounce) bags fresh spinach
1 tablespoon extra-virgin olive oil
3 cloves garlic, minced
1 (19-ounce) can chick-peas, drained and rinsed
¼ teaspoon red pepper flakes, or to taste
1 cup shredded fontina cheese

**1.** Cook the pasta until al dente according to package instructions. Add the spinach. Using a measuring cup, scoop out ½ cup of the cooking water. Immediately drain the pasta and spinach.

**2.** Meanwhile, heat the oil in a skillet over medium high. Add the garlic and cook, stirring, for 2 minutes. Add the chick-peas and red pepper flakes, cook for 1 minute, and remove from heat.

**3.** Combine the pasta mixture, chick-peas and fontina cheese in a large bowl. Stir in the reserved cooking water, and serve immediately.

**Nutritional Analysis**
For each serving: 563 calories; 25 g. protein; 81 g. carbohydrates; 13 g. dietary fiber; 16 g. fat; 6 g. saturated fat; 31 mg. cholesterol, 589 mg. sodium.

**SERVING SUGGESTION**
Serve tricolor salad with grapes: Combine arugula, radicchio and endive with sliced radishes and grapes. Dress with a light Dijon vinaigrette of 1 to 2 tablespoons balsamic vinegar, 3 tablespoons extra-virgin olive oil, ½ teaspoon Dijon mustard or to taste, and salt and pepper to taste.

**SERVES 4**

# Spinach Fettuccine with Olives, Basil and Provolone

Fresh basil is now available year round in most grocery stores. If by some chance you can't get it, don't substitute dried basil. Use fresh arugula or watercress instead.

## You Will Need

8 ounces spinach fettuccine
1 tablespoon extra-virgin olive oil
4 cloves garlic, minced
1½ pounds tomatoes,
  chopped in ½-inch pieces
½ cup kalamata olives,
  pitted and roughly chopped
1½ cups lightly packed fresh basil,
  chopped
1 cup shredded sharp provolone cheese

**1.** Cook the pasta according to package instructions. Drain but do not rinse.

**2.** Meanwhile, heat the oil in a large, nonstick skillet over medium high. Add the garlic, and cook for 1 minute. Add the tomatoes, and cook for 3 more minutes.

**3.** Toss the tomatoes in a large bowl with the olives and basil. Add the cheese and pasta, toss, and serve immediately.

### Nutritional Analysis
For each serving: 370 calories; 15 g. protein; 42 g. carbohydrates; 4 g. dietary fiber; 17.4 g. fat; 5.6 g. saturated fat; 20 mg. cholesterol, 667 mg. sodium.

### SERVING SUGGESTIONS
Accompany with steamed green beans dressed with orange juice and a dash of olive oil.
  Also, serve with semolina bread.

**SERVES 4**

# Fusilli with Mozzarella and Wilted Watercress

## COOKING:

Don't rinse cooked pasta. Not only will your pasta taste watery, but you'll remove the starchy coating that helps the sauce adhere to it.

It's amazing how much you can change a dish just by cutting the ingredients differently. When you toss hot pasta with shredded mozzarella, the cheese is dispersed throughout the dish and coats almost every piece of pasta. In this dish, the mozzarella is diced and so it doesn't melt as easily; rather than tasting it in every bite, you get the surprise of a small chunk of creaminess now and then.

## You Will Need

3 tablespoons extra-virgin olive oil
2 cloves garlic, minced
1 (28-ounce) can whole plum tomatoes, roughly chopped in their juices
¼ cup red wine
½ teaspoon salt, or to taste
⅛ teaspoon pepper
½ teaspoon thyme
½ teaspoon oregano
1 pound fusilli
½ cup pitted olives, such as kalamata, chopped
2 cups watercress leaves
4 ounces part-skim mozzarella, cut in ½-inch dice

**1.** Heat the oil in a large saucepan over medium. Add the garlic and cook, stirring, for 2 minutes, or until just golden. Add the tomatoes, wine, salt, pepper, thyme and oregano, and simmer for 15 minutes.

**2.** Meanwhile, cook the pasta according to package instructions. Drain but do not rinse.

**3.** Combine the olives and watercress in a bowl. Add the hot pasta and toss until the watercress is wilted from the heat. Stir in the sauce and the diced mozzarella, and serve immediately.

**Nutritional Analysis**
For each serving: 416 calories; 16 g. protein; 57 g. carbohydrates; 4 g. dietary fiber; 14 g. fat; 3.7 g. saturated fat; 10 mg. cholesterol, 749 mg. sodium.

**SERVING SUGGESTIONS**
Accompany with mini-pesto pizzas: Cut refrigerated pizza crust (the kind sold in tubes) into 3-inch circles (use a cookie or biscuit cutter) and bake for 5 to 7 minutes. Spread with prepared pesto, top with thin strips of roasted peppers and bake 3 to 5 minutes.

Also, serve a salad of romaine lettuce, shredded carrot, bean sprouts, sliced radishes, roughly chopped parsley leaves, dressed with a light Dijon vinaigrette: 1 to 2 tablespoons balsamic vinegar, 3 tablespoons extra-virgin olive oil, ½ teaspoon Dijon mustard or to taste, and salt and pepper to taste.

**SERVES 6**

# Pasta Puttanesca with Cannellini Beans

Everyone has an opinion about anchovies — people love them or hate them. Even if you despise them, you may find them to be a surprisingly useful addition to certain dishes. When finely minced, their strong flavor dissipates throughout the dish and you truly don't know you're eating anchovies. They add richness and a depth of flavor even when their presence isn't obvious. I prefer the anchovies that come in jars to the less expensive tinned ones, which tend to be more fishy.

## You Will Need

1 tablespoon extra-virgin olive oil
1 onion, chopped
4 cloves garlic, minced
3 anchovies, minced
2 tablespoons red wine vinegar
2 teaspoons dried basil
1 tablespoon tomato paste
1 (28-ounce) can whole plum tomatoes
½ cup pitted green olives, chopped
1 tablespoon capers
12 ounces spaghetti
1 (15-ounce) can cannellini beans, drained and rinsed
¼ to ½ teaspoon red pepper flakes

**1.** Heat the oil in a large skillet over medium high. Add the onion and garlic and cook, stirring, for 3 to 4 minutes, or until soft. Add the anchovies and saute until completely blended, about 2 more minutes.

**2.** Add the vinegar, basil, tomato paste, tomatoes, olives and capers, and bring the mixture to a boil. Reduce the heat to medium and cook for 15 minutes. Stir in the beans and pepper flakes, and cook 3 more minutes.

**3.** Meanwhile, cook the spaghetti until al dente according to package instructions. Drain but do not rinse. Toss the sauce with the pasta and serve immediately.

**Nutritional Analysis**
For each serving: 539 calories; 19.4 g. protein; 96 g. carbohydrates; 13.9 g. dietary fiber; 8.6 g. fat; 1.1 g. saturated fat; 2.6 mg. cholesterol, 1179 mg. sodium.

**SERVING SUGGESTION**
Accompany with an antipasto platter: Make a light Dijon vinaigrette of 1 to 2 tablespoons balsamic vinegar, 3 tablespoons extra-virgin olive oil, ½ teaspoon Dijon mustard or to taste, and salt and pepper to taste. Then slice mushrooms and marinate them in some of the vinaigrette for at least 20 minutes. Blanch green beans. Arrange mushrooms and beans on an oversized platter with prepared roasted red peppers, black olives and cherry tomatoes. Use remaining vinaigrette to dress the rest of the platter.

**SERVES 4**

# Penne and Vegetables with Chick-pea Vinaigrette

This vegetarian dish makes a nutritionally complete meal. Cooking the vegetables in with the pasta is a real shortcut — it takes away any worry about timing and saves a lot of cleanup.

## You Will Need

½ medium head radicchio, shredded
12 ounces penne
4 cups broccoli florets
1 medium zucchini, quartered lengthwise, then cut in ½-inch slices
1 red onion, finely chopped
2 cups cherry tomatoes, halved
1 (15-ounce) can chick-peas, rinsed and drained
1 clove garlic
1 tablespoon fresh rosemary, chopped, or 1 teaspoon dried
2 tablespoons lemon juice
½ cup water
½ teaspoon salt
⅛ teaspoon pepper
¼ cup extra-virgin olive oil
¼ cup grated Parmesan cheese

**1.** Place the radicchio in a large bowl, and set aside.

**2.** Cook the pasta according to package instructions. Add the broccoli to the pot for the last 3 minutes the pasta cooks. Add the zucchini 30 seconds later. Drain, then place the hot pasta and vegetables on top of the radicchio to wilt it. Add the onions and tomatoes, and toss.

**3.** Meanwhile, to make the vinaigrette, combine the chick-peas, garlic, rosemary, lemon juice, water, salt, pepper and olive oil in the bowl of a food processor and puree the mixture until smooth. Add the Parmesan and pulse to combine. Pour the vinaigrette over the pasta and vegetables, toss and serve.

### Nutritional Analysis

For each serving: 421 calories; 14 g. protein; 63 g. carbohydrates; 8 g. dietary fiber; 13 g. fat; 2 g. saturated fat; 3 mg. cholesterol, 350 mg. sodium.

### SERVING SUGGESTIONS

Accompany with a salad of arugula, red radish and onion dressed with a light Dijon vinaigrette: 1 to 2 tablespoons balsamic vinegar, 3 tablespoons extra-virgin olive oil, ½ teaspoon Dijon mustard or to taste, and salt and pepper to taste.

**SERVES 6**

# Farfalle with Feta

Here's a meatless dinner that has plenty of protein, carbohydrates and flavor. After you stir in the feta, let the sauce sit for a couple of minutes before you toss it with the pasta so some of the cheese melts and becomes creamy.

## You Will Need

8 ounces farfalle
1 tablespoon olive oil
½ red onion, thinly sliced
5 cloves garlic, minced
1 green pepper, cut in ½-inch dice
¼ teaspoon thyme
¼ teaspoon rosemary
½ teaspoon marjoram
1 (15-ounce) can whole tomatoes, drained
1 (15-ounce) can cannellini beans, drained and rinsed
4 ounces crumbled feta cheese
1 teaspoon lemon zest
2 tablespoons lemon juice
½ teaspoon salt
¼ teaspoon pepper

**1.** Cook the pasta according to package instructions. Drain but do not rinse.

**2.** Heat the olive oil in a skillet over medium high. Add the onion and garlic, and cook, stirring occasionally, for 5 minutes.

**3.** Add the green pepper, thyme, rosemary and marjoram, and cook for 2 minutes. Add the tomatoes and beans, and cook 2 more minutes. Remove the pan from the heat and stir in the feta cheese, lemon zest, lemon juice, salt and pepper. Let stand 2 to 3 minutes. Add the sauce to the pasta, toss and serve.

### Nutritional Analysis
For each serving: 436 calories; 17 g. protein; 63 g. carbohydrates; 7.8 g. dietary fiber; 12.9 g. fat; 6.2 g. saturated fat; 33 mg. cholesterol, 1090 mg. sodium.

### SERVING SUGGESTION
Accompany with a Greek salad: Cut romaine lettuce into 1½-inch pieces. Toss with ½ red onion thinly sliced, cherry tomatoes and 2 tablespoons chopped fresh dill. Dress with a lemon vinaigrette: 1 tablespoon lemon juice, 2 tablespoons extra-virgin olive oil, a pinch of sugar, and salt and pepper to taste.

**SERVES 4**

# Macaroni, Cheese and Tomato Casserole

## Good Idea

**FREEZER:**

Shredded cheeses sold in resealable bags keep well in the freezer. Once opened, however, store them in the refrigerator and use them up quickly. They only keep a few days once they're exposed to the air.

This dish makes a wonderful dinner for six to eight, or an easy, do-ahead side dish for a crowd of twelve or more. The recipe calls for a mixture of low-fat and full-fat Cheddar, which makes it richer than if you use just reduced-fat cheese — and you still end up with less than 30 percent of calories from fat.

## You Will Need

16 ounces elbow macaroni
2 (14½-ounce) cans diced tomatoes, drained
1 (15-ounce) can Italian-seasoned tomato sauce
2 cups shredded sharp Cheddar cheese
2 cups shredded light Cheddar cheese
¼ cup parsley, chopped (optional)

**1.** Preheat the oven to 350 degrees.

**2.** Cook the elbow macaroni until al dente according to package instructions. Drain but do not rinse.

**3.** Combine the diced tomatoes, tomato sauce and shredded cheeses in a large bowl. Add the macaroni and toss. Pour the mixture into a 9-by-13-inch baking dish. Bake for 35 to 40 minutes. Garnish with chopped parsley before serving.

**Nutritional Analysis**

For each of 8 servings: 395 calories; 22 g. protein; 48 g. carbohydrates; 4.1 g. dietary fiber; 12.3 g. fat; 7.4 g. saturated fat; 36 mg. cholesterol, 915 mg. sodium.

**SERVING SUGGESTION**

Serve with a salad of romaine lettuce, radish, cucumber, tomato, croutons, thinly sliced red onion, bottled pepperoncini peppers, black olives, shredded carrot and red pepper rings. Dress with a light red wine vinaigrette: 1 to 2 tablespoons red wine vinegar, 3 tablespoons extra-virgin olive oil, a pinch of sugar or to taste, and salt and pepper to taste.

**SERVES 8**

# Pasta with Apricots, Rosemary and Walnuts

As rich in nutrients as it is in flavor, this dish is equally good as a main course or served alongside poultry or meat. By all means make a double batch — it's great served cold. (It's also ideal for a do-ahead buffet.) Dried apricots get a little sticky when you cut them — use kitchen shears, or pile a couple on top of each other as you cut the strips and then separate them with your fingers. If you want more walnut flavor, cook the garlic mixture in 1 tablespoon of olive oil and add 2 tablespoons of walnut oil after you remove it from the heat. Be forewarned, walnut oil is fairly expensive. But it takes very little to impart a lot of nut flavor.

## You Will Need

8 ounces tagliatelle
3 tablespoons extra-virgin olive oil
2 cloves garlic, slivered
1 tablespoon fresh rosemary,
   or 1 teaspoon dried
½ cup dried apricots, cut in thin strips
½ teaspoon salt
¼ cup walnuts, roughly chopped

**1.** Cook the pasta according to package instructions. Reserve 2 tablespoons of the cooking water. Drain but do not rinse.

**2.** Place the oil, garlic, rosemary, apricots and salt in a nonstick skillet, and cook over medium until garlic is soft, about 7 minutes.

**3.** Toss the pasta with the reserved cooking water, the apricot mixture and walnuts. Serve warm or at room temperature.

**Nutritional Analysis**
For each serving: 414 calories; 9.3 g. protein; 59 g. carbohydrates; 5.6 g. dietary fiber; 15.6 g. fat; 2 g. saturated fat; 0 cholesterol, 294 mg. sodium.

**SERVING SUGGESTION**
Accompany with stuffed pitas: In a large bowl, combine 4 cups torn romaine lettuce, thinly sliced red onion, quartered cherry tomatoes, whole parsley leaves (stems removed) and 1 can drained, rinsed chick-peas. Toss with a light red wine vinaigrette: 1 to 2 tablespoons red wine vinegar, 3 tablespoons extra-virgin olive oil, a pinch of sugar or to taste, and salt and pepper to taste. Stuff salad inside individual pita breads.

**SERVES 4**

# Pasta with Shiitakes in Wild Mushroom Sauce

Dried mushrooms have a meaty flavor that makes them a perfect plant-based substitute for the confirmed carnivores in the family. Shiitakes and portobellos are available at most supermarkets, but you should also experiment with some of the more exotic mushrooms, such as oyster, lobster (named for their color, not flavor) or wood ear. Use any combination of mushrooms for this dish — no matter what you use you can't go wrong.

## You Will Need

1½ cups boiling water
½ ounce dried wild mushrooms, such as morels or porcini, rinsed
½ ounce sun-dried tomatoes (six halves), not soaked in oil, rinsed
¼ cup extra-virgin olive oil
1 medium onion, chopped
4 cloves garlic, slivered
2 teaspoons dried thyme
1 pound shiitake mushrooms, stems removed, caps cut in strips
½ cup red wine
1 (28-ounce) can whole plum tomatoes, chopped in their juices
1 pound pasta, such as farfalle or penne
½ teaspoon salt, or to taste
½ teaspoon pepper
1 cup grated Parmesan cheese, divided

**1.** Combine the boiling water, dried mushrooms and sun-dried tomatoes and set aside for 15 minutes.

**2.** Heat the oil in a large skillet over medium high. Add the onion, garlic and thyme, and cook, stirring, for 3 minutes, or until the vegetables are soft. Add the shiitakes, and cook for 2 minutes. Add the red wine and reduce the heat to medium.

**3.** Using a slotted spoon, remove the mushrooms and tomatoes from the soaking water. Chop them and add to the skillet. Slowly add the soaking liquid, being careful not to add the sediment.

**4.** Add the tomatoes, their juices, salt and pepper and simmer for 15 minutes, or until slightly thickened.

**5.** Meanwhile, cook the pasta according to the package instructions. Drain but do not rinse. Toss the pasta and sauce with ½ cup of the cheese. Serve topped with the remaining cheese.

**Nutritional Analysis**
For each serving: 510 calories; 19 g. protein; 73 g. carbohydrates; 6.6 g. dietary fiber; 16 g. fat; 4.8 g. saturated fat; 13 mg. cholesterol, 757 mg. sodium.

**SERVING SUGGESTION**
Serve with wilted spinach: In a large skillet, heat a small amount of olive oil and minced garlic over medium-high heat, about 1 minute. Place cleaned fresh spinach in the pan with only the water from rinsing clinging to its leaves. Toss the spinach as it cooks and remove the pan from the heat as soon as the leaves are wilted. Add salt and pepper to taste.

**SERVES 6**

# Pasta with Quick Ratatouille

This pasta sauce is also delicious as a side dish or as a topping for grilled chicken or fish. A classic ratatouille often includes zucchini and a variety of fresh herbs — feel free to throw them in if you have some on hand. You can also include rinsed, canned cannellini beans for added protein. Add them at the end of cooking to prevent them from getting mushy.

## You Will Need

3 tablespoons extra-virgin olive oil
3 cloves garlic, minced
1 cup sliced red onion
3 bell peppers, preferably mixed colors, cut in strips
1 tablespoon fresh thyme, or 1 teaspoon dried
10 ounces mushrooms, sliced
1 (1¼- to 1½-pound) eggplant, peeled and diced (about 2½ cups)
1½ pounds tomatoes, diced
12 ounces penne
Salt and pepper to taste

**1.** Heat the oil in a Dutch oven over medium high. Add the garlic, onion and peppers, and cook for 3 minutes. Add the thyme, mushrooms, eggplant and tomatoes, toss thoroughly and bring the mixture to a boil. Reduce the heat to simmer, cover, and cook about 20 minutes.

**2.** Meanwhile, cook the pasta according to package instructions. Drain but do not rinse. Toss the pasta with the vegetables and season to taste with salt and pepper, then serve.

**Nutritional Analysis**
For each serving: 481 calories; 14 g. protein; 80 g. carbohydrates; 9 g. dietary fiber; 13 g. fat; 1.8 g. saturated fat; 0 cholesterol, 25 mg. sodium.

**SERVING SUGGESTION**
Accompany with ham and cheese rolls: Place a thin slice of provolone cheese on top of a slice of ham and roll the two up together, jellyroll-style. Repeat to make at least 3 rolls for each person and set out on a platter with cured olives.

**SERVES 4**

# Fusilli with Beans, Caramelized Onions and Escarole

The wonderful earthy sweetness of the caramelized onion balances the mildly bitter greens in this pasta. This is a simple dish to make, and it can be easily tweaked to suit your own tastes. Try adding bits of leftover cooked meat, sauteed shrimp, or replacing the white beans with others you have on hand.

## You Will Need

8 ounces fusilli
1 head escarole, about 1 pound, leaves torn in 3-inch pieces
1 tablespoon extra-virgin olive oil
2 red onions, very thinly sliced
1 teaspoon sugar
4 cloves garlic, slivered
½ cup nonfat chicken broth
½ cup white wine
1 (15-ounce) can white beans, drained and rinsed
2 tomatoes, diced
½ teaspoon salt
½ cup grated Parmesan cheese

**1.** Cook the pasta according to package instructions. Add the escarole to the pot for the last 4 minutes the pasta cooks. Drain.

**2.** Meanwhile, heat the oil in a large skillet over medium high. Add the onions and sugar and cook, stirring, for 10 minutes, or until browned. Add the garlic, broth and wine, bring to a boil, and simmer for 5 minutes. Add the beans and tomatoes, and cook for 5 minutes. Add the salt. Toss the pasta and escarole with the sauce and Parmesan, and serve.

### Nutritional Analysis
For each serving: 451 calories; 22 g. protein; 72 g. carbohydrates; 11 g. dietary fiber; 8.8 g. fat; 3 g. saturated fat; 10 mg. cholesterol, 643 mg. sodium.

### SERVING SUGGESTION
Serve with garlic toast: Slice a baguette into ½-inch-thick slices. Rub with a cut clove of garlic, brush with olive oil, sprinkle with garlic salt and thyme, and toast in the oven until lightly crisped.

**SERVES 4**

# Fettuccine with Zucchini and Butter Beans in Lemon Garlic Sauce

This lemon sauce is substantially lower in fat than a traditional lemon pasta sauce, but it loses nothing in flavor or texture thanks to the use of a little of the pasta cooking water and grated Parmesan cheese.

## You Will Need

16 ounces fettuccine,
   spaghetti or linguine
1 (15½-ounce) can butter beans,
   drained and rinsed
6 tablespoons olive oil
5 cloves garlic, minced
2 medium zucchini,
   cut in eighths lengthwise,
   then across into 2-inch pieces
¼ cup lemon juice (2 lemons)
¾ teaspoon salt
1 teaspoon lemon zest
¼ cup grated Parmesan cheese

**1.** Cook the pasta according to package instructions. Meanwhile, drain and rinse the butter beans in a colander. When the pasta reaches the al dente stage, scoop out 1 cup of the cooking water, then drain the pasta over the beans.

**2.** Heat the oil in a large skillet over medium heat. Add the garlic, and cook for 1 minute before adding the zucchini and lemon juice. Cook for about 7 minutes, or until the zucchini is tender but not soft. Remove from the heat and stir in the pasta cooking water, salt and lemon zest. Combine the pasta and beans with the zucchini mixture, add the Parmesan cheese and toss, then serve.

### Nutritional Analysis
For each serving: 513 calories; 16 g. protein; 75 g. carbohydrates; 10 g. dietary fiber; 16.6 g. fat; 2.9 g. saturated fat; 3.3 mg. cholesterol, 526 mg. sodium.

### SERVING SUGGESTION
Accompany with tomato salad: Sprinkle sliced ripe tomatoes with a pinch of salt, drizzle with extra-virgin olive oil, and splash with balsamic vinegar. Layer in a dish with whole basil leaves. To serve, fan several slices on a plate, each topped with a basil leaf.

**SERVES 6**

# Spinach Lasagna

## Good Idea

**COOKING:**

Many sauces can be stretched or enhanced with the addition of a little of the water the pasta is cooked in. It has more body than plain water. Simply dunk a glass measuring cup into the water before you drain the pasta to retrieve some of it.

The advent of no-boil lasagna noodles was a real boon to the harried cook. If your lasagna doesn't include any ingredients that must be cooked for safety purposes, such as egg, the baking time is just a matter of softening the noodles and melding the flavors, which takes about 25 minutes. Design your own variations by including sliced precooked sausage, other vegetables, and more or less tomato sauce. Lasagna is one of my favorite one-pot suppers (although a green salad is almost mandatory).

## You Will Need

1 (10-ounce) box frozen spinach, thawed, drained and squeezed dry
½ teaspoon ground nutmeg
1 (26-ounce) jar tomato pasta sauce
6 no-boil lasagna noodles
1 (15-ounce) carton light ricotta
¾ cup shredded part-skim mozzarella
¼ cup grated Parmesan cheese

**1.** Preheat the oven to 450 degrees.

**2.** Combine the spinach and nutmeg in a bowl.

**3.** Spread ½ cup pasta sauce in the bottom of an 8-by-8-inch baking dish. Lay 2 noodles over the sauce. Top with about 1 cup ricotta, ¾ cup sauce, half the spinach, and about ¼ cup of mozzarella. Repeat the layers, ending with noodles. Spread the remaining sauce over the noodles, top with the last ¼ cup of mozzarella and sprinkle with the Parmesan. Cover with foil and bake for 25 minutes, or until bubbly. Remove the foil and bake 5 more minutes. Remove from the oven and let stand 5 minutes before serving.

### Nutritional Analysis

For each serving: 459 calories; 30 g. protein; 51 g. carbohydrates; 3.3 g. dietary fiber; 17 g. fat; 7.8 g. saturated fat; 34 mg. cholesterol, 1560 mg. sodium.

### SERVING SUGGESTIONS

Accompany with a green salad dressed with a light Dijon vinaigrette: 1 to 2 tablespoons balsamic vinegar, 3 tablespoons extra-virgin olive oil, ½ teaspoon Dijon mustard or to taste, and salt and pepper to taste.

Also, serve with garlic-oregano bread: Slice seeded semolina bread, brush with olive oil and rub with a garlic clove. Sprinkle with garlic salt and a pinch of oregano, wrap in foil and warm.

**SERVES 4**

# Asian Beef with Noodles

Don't be fooled by this long ingredients list—this recipe doesn't take long at all to throw together. What's more, this dish makes a complete, well-balanced meal, which means you don't have to worry about timing side dishes and you won't have a lot of cleanup. Frozen vegetables, which are nutritionally similar to fresh, work well in this dish and they are a great time-saver. Don't bother with the bags that include seasoning packets — you'd be paying for something you'd just end up throwing away.

## You Will Need

8 ounces spaghetti
1 tablespoon sesame oil
3 tablespoons seasoned rice vinegar
1 tablespoon lime juice
1 teaspoon minced ginger
2 cloves garlic, minced
⅛ teaspoon Asian chili paste
3 tablespoons low-sodium soy sauce
½ cup lower-sodium beef broth
1 tablespoon honey
1 pound flank steak, sliced at an angle against the grain into ¼-inch-thick slices about 2 inches long
1 pound bag frozen mixed vegetables, such as broccoli stir-fry, thawed
1 tablespoon cornstarch dissolved in 1 tablespoon water

**1.** Cook the spaghetti until al dente according to package instructions. Drain but do not rinse.

**2.** In a 2-cup measuring cup, combine the sesame oil, rice vinegar, lime juice, ginger, garlic, chili paste, soy sauce, beef broth and honey. Pour ¼ cup of the mixture into a bowl. Add the beef strips and toss.

**3.** Heat a large, nonstick skillet over medium high. Add the beef and its marinade and cook for 1½ minutes or until the meat is just cooked through. Add the frozen vegetables and cook 1½ more minutes. Add the remaining sauce mixture and the cornstarch and cook for 5 minutes, or until the vegetables are cooked through and the sauce is thickened. Toss with the cooked spaghetti and serve.

### Nutritional Analysis
For each serving: 517 calories; 36 g. protein; 62 g. carbohydrates; 7.5 g. dietary fiber; 13.6 g. fat; 4.6 g. saturated fat; 59 mg. cholesterol, 730 mg. sodium.

### SERVING SUGGESTION
Accompany with a first course of melon.

**SERVES 4**

# Pesto Shrimp with Linguine and Goat Cheese

The contrast of the herbal pesto against the tangy goat cheese gives this dish a rich flavor and yet it gets less than one-third of its calories from fat.

To make this dish even more simple, use precooked shrimp. Simply toss cooked shrimp with the pesto and proceed with the recipe. The shrimp will warm slightly when combined with the hot pasta, or you can serve this dish at room temperature.

## You Will Need

8 ounces linguine
1 teaspoon olive oil
3 cloves garlic, minced
1 pound medium shrimp, peeled
1 (3-ounce) jar prepared pesto
 (about ¼ cup)
1 to 1¼ pounds tomatoes,
 cut in ½-inch pieces
2½ ounces (about half a small log)
 goat cheese, crumbled

**1.** Cook the linguine according to package instructions. Drain but do not rinse.

**2.** Meanwhile, heat the oil in a large, nonstick skillet. Add the garlic, cook 1 minute, stirring. Add the shrimp, cook 2 minutes, turn them over, then add the pesto and cook 2 more minutes. Remove the shrimp from the pan and toss with the pasta.

**3.** Return the pan to medium heat and add the tomatoes. Cook 2 to 3 minutes, or until they are soft, and remove from heat. Add the tomatoes to the shrimp and pasta and stir in the goat cheese. Serve immediately.

**Nutritional Analysis**
For each serving: 551 calories; 39 g. protein; 57 g. carbohydrates; 4 g. dietary fiber; 19.7 g. fat; 5.6 g. saturated fat; 185 mg. cholesterol, 570 mg. sodium.

**SERVING SUGGESTION**
Accompany with a slightly bitter or peppery green salad made of arugula or watercress, with thinly sliced radishes and a citrus vinaigrette: 2 tablespoons orange juice, 1 tablespoon sherry or apple cider vinegar, 3 tablespoons extra-virgin olive oil, and salt and pepper to taste.

**SERVES 4**

# Pasta with White Clam Sauce

I loved my mother's linguine with clam sauce, and thought most restaurant versions were too oily. I was amazed when I learned my mother used canned clams, and thrilled when I learned how easy this dish is to make. Be sure to drain the liquid from the clams and use bottled clam juice — I tested this using the liquid from the can, and it was briny and fishy tasting. Bottled clam juice imparts a far fresher flavor.

## You Will Need

16 ounces perciatelli (hollow thin tubes), or other strand pasta
6 cloves garlic, sliced
¼ cup olive oil
2 (8-ounce) bottles clam juice
1 teaspoon dried basil
½ teaspoon red pepper flakes
2 (10-ounce) cans baby clams, drained
1 tablespoon lemon juice
1 cup parsley leaves, chopped
¼ cup grated Parmesan cheese

**1.** Cook the pasta according to package instructions. Drain but do not rinse.

**2.** Combine the garlic and oil in a saucepan and heat over medium for about 5 minutes, or until the garlic turns golden. Add the clam juice, basil and red pepper flakes, and cook for 3 minutes. Add the clams and lemon juice, and cook for 1 minute, or until the clams are warmed through. Toss the sauce with the pasta, parsley and Parmesan, and serve immediately.

**Nutritional Analysis**
For each serving: 497 calories; 28 g. protein; 67 g. carbohydrates; 3 g. dietary fiber; 12.6 g. fat; 2.3 g. saturated fat; 72 mg. cholesterol, 903 mg. sodium.

**SERVING SUGGESTIONS**
Serve with semolina bread.
   Also, serve wilted escarole: Wash escarole, but do not dry. Heat a large skillet over medium high, add escarole and toss continually until wilted and bright green. Remove from heat and sprinkle with lemon juice, extra-virgin olive oil, and salt and pepper to taste.

**SERVES 6**

# Shrimp on Spinach Fettuccine

Since we eat with our eyes as well as our mouths, it's worth pointing out that this is a very pretty dish, with its colors of red and green.

## You Will Need

8 ounces spinach fettuccine
2 tablespoons olive oil
1 onion, chopped
2 cloves garlic, minced
1½ pounds tomatoes, diced
1 tablespoon balsamic vinegar
½ teaspoon thyme
½ teaspoon salt
¼ teaspoon pepper
1 pound medium shrimp, peeled

**1.** Cook the fettuccine until al dente according to package instructions. Drain but do not rinse.

**2.** Meanwhile, heat the oil in a large skillet over medium high. Add the onion and garlic, and cook for 2 minutes. Add the tomatoes, vinegar, thyme, salt and pepper and cook, stirring occasionally, for 5 minutes. Add the shrimp and cook, stirring occasionally, for 5 minutes, or until the shrimp just become opaque. Toss the shrimp and vegetables with the fettuccine, and serve immediately.

### Nutritional Analysis
For each serving: 390 calories; 31 g. protein; 45 g. carbohydrates; 4.3 g. dietary fiber; 10.6 g. fat; 1.4 g. saturated fat; 172 mg. cholesterol, 578 mg. sodium.

### SERVING SUGGESTION
Serve with spinach, orange and almond salad: Toss together fresh spinach (if your store carries it, buy the baby organic spinach, which is particularly tasty and tender), drained Mandarin orange segments, thinly sliced red onion and slivered almonds. Use 1 teaspoon of the syrup from the Mandarin oranges to sweeten a dressing made of 2 tablespoons raspberry vinegar, 3 tablespoons extra-virgin olive oil, and thyme, salt and pepper to taste.

**SERVES 4**

# Peanut Noodles with Pork

Pork tenderloin is very lean. In fact, it's nutritional profile is similar to that of skinless chicken breast. Don't worry if the tenderloin at your market is slightly smaller than the recipe calls for: There's plenty of protein in this dish from the peanut butter, and you'll certainly still have large enough portions. This dish is also great cold, so make a double batch if you want to have it two nights — just don't double the chili paste, or the dish will be too fiery.

## You Will Need

¼ cup hoisin sauce
¼ cup natural-style chunky peanut butter
2 tablespoons seasoned rice vinegar
¼ cup nonfat chicken broth
⅛ teaspoon Asian chili paste, or to taste
1 pound boneless pork tenderloin,
    cut crosswise into ¼-inch-thick slices
8 ounces vermicelli, spaghetti or linguine
4 cups broccoli florets
1 red pepper, cut in strips
2 teaspoons peanut or canola oil
4 to 5 scallions, cut across in thin slices

**1.** Combine the hoisin sauce, peanut butter, rice vinegar, chicken broth and chili paste. Toss 2 tablespoons of the mixture with the pork and set aside the remaining mixture.

**2.** Cook the pasta according to package instructions. Add the broccoli to the pot the last 4 minutes the pasta cooks. When the broccoli is bright green after about 2 minutes, add the red pepper to the pot. Drain the pasta and vegetables.

**3.** Meanwhile, heat the oil in a nonstick skillet. Add the pork and cook for 4 minutes, stirring occasionally, or until it's no longer pink in the middle. Add the remaining sauce to the pan, and cook for 1 more minute. Toss the pasta and vegetables with the pork. Top with the chopped scallions and serve.

### Nutritional Analysis
For each serving: 524 calories; 37 g. protein; 55 g. carbohydrates; 9.8 g. dietary fiber; 18 g. fat; 3 g. saturated fat; 75 mg. cholesterol, 587 mg. sodium.

### SERVING SUGGESTION
This dish has all the components of a complete meal, but a light crunchy side dish of jicama sticks would offer a refreshing contrast. Simply peel the jicama, cut it into ¼-inch matchsticks and sprinkle with salt. Jicama has a mildly sweet, slightly nutty flavor.

**SERVES 4**

# Sausage with Apples and Caramelized Onions over Egg Noodles

This is a homey autumnal dish that takes advantage of just harvested apples. If you can't get apple-flavored chicken sausage, use any mild, sweet turkey or chicken sausage and replace half the chicken broth with apple juice. Golden Delicious apples are usually the apple I choose for cooking, because they stand up particularly well in flavor and texture to heat. Granny Smith, with their appealing tart flavor, also work in this dish.

## You Will Need

8 ounces very wide egg noodles
2 teaspoons olive oil
12 ounces precooked apple-flavored
   chicken sausage, sliced in ½-inch
   pieces
2 medium onions, thinly sliced
2 medium apples, peeled and cut into
   ½-inch wedges
1 teaspoon apple cider vinegar
½ teaspoon salt
½ cup nonfat chicken broth

**1.** Cook the noodles according to package instructions. Drain but do not rinse.

**2.** Meanwhile, heat the oil in a large, nonstick skillet. Add the sausage and onions and cook over medium high, stirring, for 4 minutes. Add the apple slices and cook for 2 more minutes. Add the vinegar and salt, and cook until the onions brown, about 4 minutes. Add the broth, cover, reduce heat to medium, and cook for 10 minutes. Divide the noodles among 4 plates, top with the sausage mixture and serve immediately.

**Nutritional Analysis**
For each serving: 460 calories; 23 g. protein; 59 g. carbohydrates; 6.4 g. dietary fiber; 15.6 g. fat; 3.9 g. saturated fat; 130 mg. cholesterol, 917 mg. sodium.

**SERVING SUGGESTIONS**
Serve with butternut squash: Peel squash, cut into small cubes, boil until tender and toss with nutmeg, salt, plenty of ground black pepper and a squeeze of lemon juice.

Also, serve braised Savoy cabbage: Cut cabbage in wedges and place in a large skillet in about 1 inch of nonfat chicken broth. Sprinkle with salt and caraway seeds, cover the pot and cook over medium heat until cabbage is just tender, about 10 minutes.

**SERVES 4**

# Lemon Penne with Sausage and Spinach

The fact that this dish is colorful not only means it's pleasing to the eye, but that it's full of a variety of nutrients. The color of produce is indicative of the type of nutrient it contains, so you ensure consumption of a range of vitamins and minerals by eating a dish containing many colors.

## You Will Need

8 ounces penne
1 small yellow squash (about ½ pound) cut in half lengthwise, then sliced
3 to 4 ounces uncooked chicken or turkey sausage (1 link)
1 onion, chopped
1 cup nonfat chicken broth
2 tablespoons olive oil
½ teaspoon fennel seeds
4 cups packed fresh spinach (preferably baby spinach)
1 cup cherry tomatoes, cut in half
1 tablespoon lemon juice
½ teaspoon salt
¼ teaspoon pepper
¼ cup grated Parmesan cheese

**1.** Cook the pasta according to package instructions. Add the yellow squash to the pot for the last 3 minutes the pasta cooks. Drain and set aside.

**2.** Meanwhile, squeeze the sausage out of its casing and into a large, nonstick skillet. Cook over medium high for 3 minutes, constantly stirring to break it into bits. Add the onion to the pan and cook, stirring, 2 minutes. Add the chicken broth, olive oil and fennel seeds, and boil for 2 minutes. Add the spinach and cherry tomatoes and remove the pan from the heat. Stir in the lemon juice, salt and pepper. Toss the pasta in the skillet with the sausage mixture. Stir in the Parmesan, and serve immediately.

### Nutritional Analysis

For each serving: 414 calories; 18 g. protein; 57 g. carbohydrates; 5 g. dietary fiber; 13 g. fat; 3 g. saturated fat; 26 mg. cholesterol, 770 mg. sodium.

### SERVING SUGGESTION

Accompany with quick bean soup: Combine drained and rinsed canned cannellini beans, chicken broth, chopped carrot, celery and onion and dried thyme in a saucepan and cook over medium heat until vegetables are soft. Remove half the mixture from pot and puree it in a blender or food processor. Ladle puree back into the soup pot and reheat it. After ladling soup into serving bowls, drizzle with extra-virgin olive oil.

## Good Idea

**COOKING:**
If your pasta clumps, you probably aren't cooking it in enough water. Every pound of pasta should roll around in 4 quarts of boiling water. And be sure to add a little salt just before adding the pasta. Even if you're trying to cut down on your sodium intake, don't skip this step. The salt enhances the flavor of the pasta, and most of it drains off with the cooking water.

# Creamy Pasta Primavera

This dish makes a complete, rich meal (that gets only 26 percent of its calories from fat). Vary the vegetables with whatever looks good or happens to be on sale at the grocery store. Also, to cut the fat, calories and sodium, or to simply use up leftovers, replace the bacon with any cooked poultry or meat.

When using sour cream, don't subject it to direct heat, or it will break down into unsightly lumps. When it's warmed indirectly, as it is in this dish, it gives sauces a wonderful creaminess.

## You Will Need

8 ounces medium shell pasta
4 cups broccoli florets
1 medium zucchini, cut lengthwise in eighths, then across in ½-inch pieces
½ pound Canadian-style bacon, diced
½ cup light sour cream
2 tablespoons milk
½ cup grated Parmesan cheese
2 cups cherry tomatoes, halved
1 (7-ounce) jar roasted red peppers, drained and cut in ½-inch pieces

**1.** Cook the pasta according to package instructions. Add the broccoli to the pot for the last 5 minutes the pasta cooks, then add the zucchini for the last 2 minutes. Drain.

**2.** Meanwhile, place the bacon in a nonstick pan, heat and cook for 5 minutes, or until lightly browned. Remove the pan from the heat, stir in the sour cream, milk and cheese. Toss the pasta and vegetables with the bacon mixture, tomatoes and roasted peppers, and serve immediately.

### Nutritional Analysis
For each serving: 421 calories; 28 g. protein; 51 g. carbohydrates; 4.9 g. dietary fiber; 12 g. fat; 5.6 g. saturated fat; 49 mg. cholesterol, 1265 mg. sodium.

### SERVING SUGGESTION
Serve with a salad of crisp romaine, thinly sliced red onion, cucumber and radishes dressed with a light Dijon vinaigrette: 1 to 2 tablespoons balsamic vinegar, 3 tablespoons extra-virgin olive oil, ½ teaspoon Dijon mustard or to taste, and salt and pepper to taste.

**SERVES 4**

# Baked Penne Bolognese

..........................................................................................................

I use ground turkey instead of beef to reduce the fat in this universally well-liked pasta dinner. If you also need to watch your sodium, read labels and buy a low- or no-salt tomato sauce. (You could do that, add some salt to taste, and still end up with a lower sodium dish.) If you're in a hurry, skip baking the dish, and serve it with the cheese not quite melted — it's still delicious.

## You Will Need

8 ounces penne
1 tablespoon olive oil
1 onion, chopped
2 cloves garlic, minced
½ teaspoon dried oregano
½ teaspoon dried basil
½ teaspoon dried thyme
½ teaspoon salt
¾ pound lean (93 percent fat-free) ground turkey
1 cup sliced mushrooms
2 (15-ounce) cans tomato sauce
1 cup shredded light mozzarella
¼ cup grated Parmesan cheese

**1.** Preheat the oven to 450 degrees. Coat a large baking dish with cooking spray.

**2.** Cook the pasta until al dente according to package instructions. Drain but do not rinse.

**3.** Heat the oil in a large skillet over medium high. Add the onion and garlic and cook, stirring, for 2 minutes, or until softened. Add the oregano, basil, thyme, salt, turkey and mushrooms and cook, stirring, about 3 minutes, or until the turkey is no longer pink. Add the tomato sauce, reduce the heat to medium and cook for 15 minutes.

**4.** Combine the sauce and pasta. Place in the baking dish and top with the mozzarella and Parmesan cheeses. Bake for 15 minutes, or until the mozzarella is melted.

### Nutritional Analysis
For each serving: 521 calories; 38 g. protein; 58 g. carbohydrates; 16 g. fat; 6 g. saturated fat; 68 mg. cholesterol, 1957 mg. sodium.

### SERVING SUGGESTION
Serve with romaine salad: Combine romaine lettuce, croutons, thinly sliced red onion, capers and halved cherry tomatoes and dress with creamy buttermilk mustard vinaigrette: 1 tablespoon vinegar, ½ teaspoon Dijon mustard, 1 tablespoon extra-virgin olive oil, ¼ cup low-fat buttermilk, ½ teaspoon sugar and pepper to taste.

**SERVES 4**

# Wagon Wheel Pasta with Turkey Meat Sauce

This is the ultimate kid-friendly meal. Not only do children get a kick out of the wagon wheel-shaped pasta, it's easy for them to eat. Using turkey instead of beef makes this a healthier version of classic meat sauce. You can vary it by adding a pinch of rosemary or red pepper flakes.

## You Will Need

2 teaspoons oil
1 onion, chopped
2 cloves garlic, minced
1 teaspoon dried oregano
¾ pound lean (93 percent fat-free) ground turkey
½ teaspoon salt
⅛ teaspoon ground black pepper
1 (15-ounce) can whole plum tomatoes, chopped in their juices
1 (15-ounce) can crushed tomatoes
8 ounces wagon wheel-shaped pasta
½ cup light shredded Cheddar or Monterey Jack cheese

**1.** Heat the oil in a large skillet over medium high. Add the onion, garlic and oregano and cook, stirring, for 2 minutes. Add the turkey, salt and pepper, and cook for 3 minutes, stirring to break up the meat. Add the chopped and crushed tomatoes, reduce the heat to medium and cook for 15 minutes.

**2.** Meanwhile, cook the pasta until al dente according to package instructions. Drain but do not rinse. Combine the pasta and sauce. Divide among plates and top each serving with 2 tablespoons of the cheese.

### Nutritional Analysis

For each serving: 449 calories; 31 g. protein; 52 g. carbohydrates; 5.2 g. dietary fiber; 12.3 g. fat; 3.8 g. saturated fat; 73 mg. cholesterol, 869 mg. sodium.

### SERVING SUGGESTION

Serve with asparagus: Place asparagus flat in a large skillet. Add about ½-inch water. Bring to a boil and cook until asparagus just turns bright green. Drain and sprinkle with lemon juice and salt.

**SERVES 4**

# Pasta with Salsa Cruda

Salsa cruda means fresh sauce. You don't cook the sauce for this dish. Use only very ripe tomatoes, which soften slightly from the heat of the pasta. The packages of chopped Italian-seasoned cooked chicken breast available in the meat case of the supermarket are perfect for this dish, though any cooked chicken will do.

## You Will Need

1½ pounds tomatoes, chopped
1 clove garlic, minced
½ small red onion, very thinly sliced
1 tablespoon red wine vinegar
2 tablespoons olive oil
1 teaspoon salt
¼ teaspoon pepper
½ cup loosely packed basil,
    cut into thin strips or roughly chopped
8 ounces rotini
10 ounces cooked chicken
    (about 2 cups), cut into bite-size pieces
¼ cup grated Parmesan cheese

**1.** Combine the tomatoes, garlic, onion, vinegar, oil, salt, pepper and basil.

**2.** Cook the pasta according to package instructions. Drain but do not rinse. Toss with the chicken and the tomato mixture. Top each serving with 1 tablespoon of the Parmesan.

### Nutritional Analysis

For each serving: 458 calories; 32 g. protein; 47 g. carbohydrates; 4.2 g. dietary fiber; 15.6 g. fat; 3.9 g. saturated fat; 64 mg. cholesterol, 766 mg. sodium.

### SERVING SUGGESTION

Accompany with steamed green beans tossed with balsamic vinegar and extra-virgin olive oil.

## Good Idea

**SHOPPING:**
The best way to select a tomato is with your nose. Take a deep whiff at the stem end of a ripe tomato and you'll smell what can only be described as a strong tomato perfume. Don't buy perfect-looking tomatoes. Those brown and dark green lines that run down the sides are a sign that the fruit was allowed to ripen on the vine — which means it will be more flavorful. As for shape, just as with humans, a perfectly shaped exterior is no sign of what's below the surface.

**SERVES 4**

# Meatless Meals

*Experience a taste of Tex-Mex with Vegetarian Enchiladas*

# Aromatic Apricot Couscous and Chick-peas

The sweetness of dried apricots and orange juice is balanced with the salty and earthy bite of capers and cumin to make this couscous an addictive meatless meal. This dish is equally good served hot or cold.

## You Will Need

**FOR THE COUSCOUS:**
¾ cup orange juice
¾ cup nonfat chicken broth
   (or vegetable broth)
1 bay leaf
1 cup couscous
**FOR THE CHICK-PEAS:**
1 tablespoon extra-virgin olive oil
1 red pepper, diced
1 small onion, chopped
1 teaspoon cumin seed
½ teaspoon ground ginger
1 (15-ounce) can chick-peas,
   rinsed and drained
½ cup diced dried apricots
2 tablespoons capers
½ cup cilantro, chopped
½ cup fresh mint, chopped
3 scallions, chopped
Salt to taste

**1.** Bring the orange juice, broth and bay leaf to a boil. Add the couscous, cover and remove from heat. Let it stand at least 5 minutes, or until the liquid is fully absorbed. Set aside.

**2.** Heat the oil in a skillet. Add the red pepper, onion, cumin, ginger, chick-peas, apricots and capers, and cook, stirring occasionally, 6 minutes, or until the vegetables are soft.

**3.** Combine the chick-pea mixture with the couscous, cilantro, mint and scallions and season to taste with salt.

**Nutritional Analysis**
For each serving: 389 calories; 12 g. protein; 73 g. carbohydrates; 12 g. dietary fiber; 6.4 g. fat; <1 g. saturated fat; 0 cholesterol, 521 mg. sodium.

**SERVING SUGGESTION**
Serve this couscous on a bed of raw spinach leaves tossed with a light vinaigrette made of 3 tablespoons olive oil, 2 tablespoons vinegar and a generous pinch of sugar.

**SERVES 4**

# Black Bean, Corn and Tomato Salad

This simple recipe makes a salad with complex layers of flavor that packs a nutritional punch. It's high in fiber and carbohydrates, low in saturated fat and has no cholesterol and offers a hefty serving of phytochemicals — the nutrients in plants thought to help prevent cancer, heart disease and many other illnesses.

## You Will Need

2 ears of corn
½ cup frozen peas
1 (15-ounce) can black beans, drained and rinsed
½ small red onion, diced
2 medium beefsteak tomatoes, cut in ¼-inch dice
2 tablespoons orange juice
1 tablespoon sherry vinegar
½ teaspoon salt
½ teaspoon cumin
½ teaspoon coriander
3 tablespoons extra-virgin olive oil

**1.** Cook corn in boiling water for about 2 minutes, remove, then add peas. Cook peas until tender, about 4 more minutes. Drain.

**2.** Cut kernels off the cob and combine with black beans, peas, red onion and tomatoes.

**3.** To make the dressing, whisk together the orange juice, vinegar, salt, cumin, coriander and olive oil. Pour dressing over the bean mixture, and toss lightly to serve.

**Nutritional Analysis**
For each serving: 254 calories; 9 g. protein; 32 g. carbohydrates; 9 g. dietary fiber; 11.8 g. fat; 1.5 g. saturated fat; 0 cholesterol, 648 mg. sodium.

**SERVING SUGGESTIONS**
Serve beans simply on a bed of Romaine lettuce, accompanied by crusty French or sourdough bread, or serve stuffed in pita bread with lettuce leaves.

For a more elaborate presentation that can be put together in less than 15 minutes:

• Cut the top ½ inch off 4 large beefsteak tomatoes. Scoop out the insides and fill them with the bean mixture. (If the tomato is meaty enough, you can add some of it to the bean mixture, or reserve it to add to pasta sauce.)

• Cut 2 medium zucchini in half lengthwise, scoop out the insides and lightly steam or microwave until just tender. Fill with the bean mixture.

• Bake 4 yellow or red peppers until tender, scoop out seeds and fill with the bean mixture.

**SERVES 4**

# Vegetarian Enchiladas

Traditional enchiladas are made with steamed or fried corn tortillas. This easy-to-prepare dish uses flour tortillas and cuts out the fat you'd use to fry the corn ones.

These enchiladas evolved from an inadvertent pun made by my son Zach. One day he commented that he wished I would make plain burritos, but he thought they counted as junk food. I explained they are not junk food at all, and he was amazed. Turns out he meant "plane" burritos, like the ones he had eaten on a recent flight to his grandmother's house.

## You Will Need

4 low-fat, burrito-sized flour tortillas
1 (16-ounce) can fat-free refried beans
1 cup canned whole kernel corn
1 (10-ounce) can diced tomatoes
   with green chiles
2 cups shredded light Cheddar cheese
1 cup mild enchilada sauce

**1.** Preheat the oven to 400 degrees.

**2.** Warm the tortillas according to package directions. Working one at a time, place ½ cup of the refried bean mixture in a strip down the center of the tortilla, leaving a 1-inch border at the top and bottom. Top with ¼ cup of the corn and a scant ¼ cup of the tomato and green chile mixture. Sprinkle with ¼ cup of shredded cheese. Fold one side in toward the center, then roll the tortilla up tightly and place seam side down in a baking dish. Repeat with the remaining ingredients.

**3.** Pour the enchilada sauce over the rolled tortillas, top with remaining grated cheese and bake for 15 to 20 minutes, or until the cheese is melted and the enchiladas are warmed through. Serve immediately.

### Nutritional Analysis
For each serving: 502 calories; 26.6 g. protein; 73.5 g. carbohydrates; 8.7 g. dietary fiber; 10.5 g. fat; 3.3 g. saturated fat; 12 mg. cholesterol, 1743 mg. sodium.

### SERVING SUGGESTIONS
Serve with baked tortilla chips and a salad of Romaine lettuce and tomato tossed with a cumin vinaigrette: Combine 3 tablespoons olive oil, 2 tablespoons red wine vinegar, a generous pinch of sugar and a dash of cumin.

**SERVES 4**

# Cream of Potato and Fennel Soup

This is comfort food at its best: Thick, creamy warm soup with just enough flavor so that you can taste it even with a cold, but not so much that it assaults your palate. I also appreciate anything this low in fat and calories that is so delicious and easy.

You can make this soup in a food processor, or with one of my favorite kitchen tools — the immersion blender. This relatively inexpensive appliance lets you cream and puree soups and vegetables right in the pot they were cooked in, saving you the hassle of working in batches with a food processor.

## You Will Need

1 bulb fennel, trimmed and
  cut in large chunks
½ medium onion, cut in large chunks
1 tablespoon olive oil
4 medium potatoes, peeled and
  cut in ½-inch pieces
2 (14½-ounce) cans nonfat chicken broth
  (or vegetable broth)
2 cups skim milk
½ teaspoon salt
⅛ teaspoon black pepper

**1.** Place the fennel and onion in a food processor bowl and mince to about ¼-inch pieces.

**2.** Heat the oil in a large saucepan over medium high. Add the fennel and onion; cook about 4 minutes, or until the vegetables soften. Add the potatoes and broth and bring to a boil. Cover the pan and boil for 15 minutes, or until potatoes are soft. Add milk, salt and pepper; cook another 2 minutes, or until the mixture is sufficiently hot.

**3.** Working in batches, puree the mixture in the bowl of a food processor (or in the saucepan with an immersion blender). Return the soup to the saucepan and keep it warm until serving.

### Nutritional Analysis
For each serving: 240 calories; 8.8 g. protein; 43.7 g. carbohydrates; 5 g. dietary fiber; 3.9 g. fat; <1 g. saturated fat; 2 mg. cholesterol, 942 mg. sodium.

### SERVING SUGGESTIONS
Accompany with toasted French bread rounds spread with tapenade (olive spread): Combine finely minced garlic, pitted kalamata olives in the bowl of a food processor. With the machine running, slowly add extra-virgin olive oil until the mixture is the consistency of paste.

Also serve an arugula or watercress salad served with light Dijon vinaigrette: Combine 3 tablespoons olive oil, 2 tablespoons vinegar, a generous pinch of sugar and Dijon mustard to taste.

**SERVES 4**

# Cuban Black Beans and Rice

**NUTRITION:**
Rinsing canned beans not only makes them taste better, but it cuts their sodium content by about one-third. You can reduce the amount of sodium listed in the nutritional information at the bottom of the recipes in this book that use beans by rinsing them before using.

Just reading this recipe doesn't tell you how great this dish is. It's inexpensive and easy to make, and tastes even better after a day or two. I like to make a double batch and turn the leftovers into burritos, puree them with chicken broth to make soup, or continue eating them as made, hot or cold.

## You Will Need

1 cup white rice
1 tablespoon olive oil
2 cloves garlic, minced
1 teaspoon dried oregano
1 teaspoon ground cumin
⅛ teaspoon black pepper
1 green or orange pepper, cut in ½-inch pieces
1 cup frozen corn
1 (14 ½-ounce) can whole plum tomatoes, chopped in their juices
1 tablespoon red wine vinegar
1 (15-ounce) can black beans, drained and rinsed
Salt and pepper to taste

**1.** Cook the rice according to package directions.

**2.** Heat the oil over medium high in a large saucepan or skillet. Add garlic, oregano, cumin, black pepper, diced pepper and corn, stirring to break up the frozen corn. Lower heat to medium, add tomatoes and vinegar, and cook 10 minutes.

**3.** Stir in the beans and cook 7 more minutes, or until beans are heated through. Season to taste with salt and pepper and serve over a bed of the white rice.

### Nutritional Analysis
For each serving: 347 calories; 11.7 g. protein; 77 g. carbohydrates; 9 g. dietary fiber; 5 g. fat; <1 g. saturated fat; 0 cholesterol, 491 mg. sodium.

### SERVING SUGGESTIONS
Serve with baked tortilla chips and a green salad tossed with Dijon vinaigrette: Combine 3 tablespoons olive oil, 2 tablespoons red wine vinegar, a generous pinch of sugar and Dijon mustard to taste.

**SERVES 4**

# Leek and Spinach Frittata

This version of the Italian omelet has a fraction of the fat and cholesterol of a traditional frittata. A large serving — one fourth of the pie — has only 195 calories and 8.5 grams of fat.

To use leeks, discard the green leaves. Cut the white in half lengthwise, then across in thin slices. Place the slices in a colander and rinse under cold water, tossing several times.

## You Will Need
2 teaspoons extra-virgin olive oil
4 cups sliced leeks (about 4 medium size)
1 red pepper, diced
2 cups packed baby spinach
3 large eggs
6 large egg whites
½ teaspoon salt
¼ teaspoon pepper
½ teaspoon thyme
¼ cup crumbled feta cheese

**1.** Preheat the broiler. Cover the handle of a 10-inch, nonstick skillet with foil if it isn't ovenproof.

**2.** Heat the oil over medium high in the skillet. Add the leeks, which will seem to overwhelm the skillet until they cook down. Cook for 12 minutes, tossing occasionally, or until the leeks are golden brown. Add the red pepper, toss, and add the spinach. Cook 2 to 3 minutes, or until the spinach is partially wilted.

**3.** While the leeks are cooking, whisk together the eggs and egg whites, salt, pepper and thyme. Pour the mixture over the cooked vegetables and stir briefly to be sure the ingredients are evenly dispersed. Let the egg mixture cook 5 to 7 minutes without stirring. When the eggs are set everywhere but on the very top of the frittata, run a butter knife around the rim and sprinkle the feta over the top.

**4.** Place the frittata under the broiler for 3 minutes, or until the cheese is melted. Cut in wedges to serve.

**Nutritional Analysis**
For each serving: 195 calories; 14 g. protein; 17 g. carbohydrates; 3 g. dietary fiber; 8.5 g. fat; 3 g. saturated fat; 168 mg. cholesterol, 558 mg. sodium.

**SERVING SUGGESTION**
Accompany with grilled cheese, tomato and watercress sandwiches: Melt Cheddar on sliced bread in the oven or toaster oven. Top with a slice of tomato and return to the oven to heat the tomato. Top with watercress and a slice of lightly buttered bread, and toast the sandwich until golden.

**SERVES 4 GENEROUSLY**

# Pasta and Chick-pea Soup

My friend Trudy Solin somehow always has a house full of hungry mouths to feed on Sundays. She never knows how many people will show up, yet she always has enough food on hand. One of her tricks is a well-stocked pantry — she can throw a delicious and hearty soup together on a moment's notice. This is an adaptation of one of her favorites. It makes a thick soup — almost a stew — that's just the thing for a crisp fall night. One note: Don't omit the anchovies, because they add a depth of flavor that is anything but fishy.

## You Will Need

¼ cup olive oil
1 stalk celery, chopped
1 carrot, chopped
1 onion, chopped
2 cloves garlic, minced
3 anchovy fillets, finely minced
½ cup chopped parsley
1 (15-ounce) can chick-peas
2 large tomatoes, chopped
2 teaspoons rosemary
2 cups nonfat chicken broth
8 ounces elbow macaroni
6 tablespoons grated Parmesan cheese

**1.** In a large saucepan, heat the oil over medium and add the celery, carrots, onion, garlic, anchovies and parsley. Cook 5 minutes.

**2.** Add the chick-peas and their liquid, tomatoes, rosemary and chicken broth. Cover and cook 20 minutes.

**3.** Meanwhile, cook the pasta in boiling water for 8 minutes. Before draining, check the soup — if it's too thick, add ¼ cup of the pasta water to thin it. Drain the pasta and add it to the soup. Cook another 5 minutes, or until pasta is tender. Ladle into bowls and serve topped with 1 tablespoon of the Parmesan cheese.

**Nutritional Analysis**
For each serving: 350 calories; 12 g. protein; 48 g. carbohydrates; 6 g. dietary fiber; 12.5 g. fat; 2.4 g. saturated fat; 8 mg. cholesterol, 717 mg. sodium.

**SERVING SUGGESTION**
Accompany with tomato-arugula toasts: Lightly toast white sandwich bread. Top it with country-style Dijon mustard, thinly sliced tomato, arugula and a slice of sharp provolone and return it to the oven or toaster oven until the cheese melts.

**SERVES 6**

# Baked Polenta Rounds with Eggplant, Tomato and Blue Cheese Topping

This meatless dinner is quite rich, thanks to the flavorful blue cheese. Precooked rolls of polenta, found in most supermarkets, will keep several months in your refrigerator.

## You Will Need

**FOR THE TOPPING:**
1 tablespoon extra-virgin olive oil
1 onion, chopped
3 cloves garlic, minced
2 pounds tomatoes, cut in 1-inch chunks
1 tablespoon fresh rosemary, chopped
1 green pepper, cut in 1-inch pieces
1 ½ pounds eggplant, peeled and
   cut in ½-inch dice
10 ounces mushrooms,
   cleaned and quartered
½ teaspoon salt
⅛ teaspoon black pepper
¾ cup crumbled blue cheese
   (about 3 ounces)

**FOR THE ROUNDS:**
1 (24-ounce) roll precooked polenta
2 tablespoons extra-virgin olive oil

**1.** To make the topping, heat the oil in a large skillet over medium high and add the onion and garlic. Cook 2 minutes, add tomatoes, rosemary, green pepper, eggplant, mushrooms, salt and pepper.

**2.** Cover, reduce the heat to medium, and cook, stirring occasionally, for 10 minutes. Remove the cover and cook another 10 to 12 minutes, or until the vegetables are soft.

**3.** Let the vegetables cool slightly, then transfer them to a bowl and stir in the blue cheese.

**4.** To make the polenta rounds, preheat the oven to 500 degrees. Coat a baking sheet with cooking spray. Cut the polenta into ½-inch slices. Brush both sides of the slices with olive oil and place on the baking sheet. Bake the rounds for 15 minutes, then turn and bake them 5 to 7 minutes more, or until they are light golden brown around the edges. Place 3 polenta rounds on each plate and top with 1½ cups of the eggplant mixture.

### Nutritional Analysis
For each serving: 435 calories; 14 g. protein; 56 g. carbohydrates; 10 g. dietary fiber; 19 g. fat; 6.4 g saturated fat; 19 mg. cholesterol, 1201 mg. sodium.

### SERVING SUGGESTIONS
Start this meal with a refreshing course of melon.

**Good Idea**

**INGREDIENTS:**
Instant polenta, which is partially cooked in a process akin to that of quick-cooking oatmeal and instant rice, requires almost no stirring. It can be used as an alternative to rice and pasta — it's another good source of low-fat carbohydrates.

**SERVES 4**

# Southwestern-Flavored Souffle Omelets

Although avocado is high in fat, it contains mostly monounsaturated fat — the heart-healthy kind. And if you watch your fat intake because of weight, notice that these omelets make a low-calorie but satisfying dinner.

## You Will Need

1 ripe avocado, peeled and
    chopped into ¼-inch pieces
1 medium tomato, cut in ¼-inch dice
½ medium cucumber, cut in ¼-inch dice
½ small red onion, cut in ¼-inch dice
Juice from 1 lime
¼ cup cilantro, chopped
½ teaspoon salt, plus a pinch
Pinch cayenne pepper (to taste)
4 large eggs
4 large egg whites
2 teaspoons olive oil, divided

**1.** Combine the avocado, tomato, cucumber, red onion, lime juice, cilantro, ½ teaspoon of salt and cayenne in a bowl and set aside.

**2.** Whisk the whole eggs until frothy. In a separate bowl, beat the egg whites and a pinch of salt until soft peaks form. Fold the egg whites into the whole eggs.

**3.** Heat 1 teaspoon of the oil in a medium-sized, nonstick skillet. Pour in half of the egg mixture and cook over medium heat, covered, for 2 minutes. Pour half the avocado mixture over the half of the omelet farthest away from the pan handle, leaving a 1-inch border from the edge, and cook 2 minutes. Fold the empty half of the omelet over the filling, let it set for about 1 minute, then slide the omelet onto the plate. Cover loosely with plastic wrap while you repeat the procedure with the remaining ingredients. To serve, cut each omelet in half and slide onto dinner plates.
   Note: Omelets can be kept hot up to 20 minutes if placed in an oven preheated to warm or low.

**Nutritional Analysis**
For each serving: 211 calories; 12 g. protein; 9 g. carbohydrates; 3.5 g. dietary fiber; 15 g. fat; 3 g. saturated fat; (8 g. monounsaturated fat); 213 mg. cholesterol, 418 mg. sodium.

**SERVING SUGGESTIONS**
Serve with a tossed green salad as well as cheese toasts: Butter or lightly brush olive oil on whole wheat bread. Top with grated Cheddar cheese, cut each slice in 4 triangles and warm in an oven or toaster oven until the cheese is just melted.

**SERVES 4**

# Vegetable and Tofu Stir-fry

After spending a week at a spa, I remembered how good it feels to eat healthful, crunchy vegetables and calcium- and protein-rich tofu. I recognize that many people are tofu-phobic — convinced that they or their families won't like it. If that's the case, use half a pound each of tofu and chicken to give this dish a try. Cut the chicken in small pieces, toss it with half the sauce, and cook it with the ginger and garlic. Proceed with the rest of the recipe as written, leaving the chicken in the wok.

## You Will Need

¼ cup hoisin sauce
¼ cup low-sodium soy sauce
½ cup water
¼ teaspoon Asian chili paste, or to taste
1 pound firm tofu, drained and cut in 1-inch cubes (or ½ pound each tofu and diced chicken breasts)
1 tablespoon sesame oil
1 tablespoon minced ginger
3 garlic cloves, minced
2 carrots, sliced
2 cups broccoli florets
1 stalk bok choy, sliced
1 cup green beans
1 yellow pepper, diced
1 small zucchini, sliced
1 tablespoon cornstarch dissolved in 1 tablespoon water

**1.** Combine the hoisin, soy sauce, water and chili paste in a bowl and toss with the tofu. Set aside.

**2.** Heat the oil in a large, nonstick skillet or wok. Add the ginger and garlic and stir-fry 1 minute. Add the carrots and broccoli and stir-fry 1 to 2 minutes. Add the bok choy, green beans, yellow pepper, zucchini and tofu mixture and stir-fry about 4 to 6 minutes, or until vegetables are just tender. Stir in cornstarch and cook, stirring until sauce is thickened, about 2 to 3 minutes. Serve immediately.

**Nutritional Analysis**
For each serving: 319 calories; 24 g. protein; 30 g. carbohydrates; 8 g. dietary fiber; 14 g. fat; 2.1 g. saturated fat; <1 mg. cholesterol, 843 mg. sodium.

**SERVING SUGGESTION**
Serve on a bed of quick-cooking brown rice.

## Good Idea

**NUTRITION:**
Tofu is often thought of as a low-fat food. It isn't, but it is a low-calorie, high-calcium source of protein. The fat it contains is the good fat — monounsaturated fat — so eat it to your heart's (and waistline's) content.

**SERVES 4**

# Tortellini in Garlic Broth

This recipe is a good example of how you can have your butter and eat low fat, too. A mere two tablespoons of butter gives the broth a creamy richness — but this dish still gets only 30 percent of its calories from fat.

## You Will Need

16 ounces frozen cheese tortellini
1 small head fresh escarole,
   about 1 pound, torn into 3-inch pieces
2 teaspoons extra-virgin olive oil
1 small onion, chopped
5 cloves garlic, thinly sliced
½ cup nonfat chicken broth
½ cup white wine
1 (15-ounce) can whole plum tomatoes,
   drained and roughly chopped
2 tablespoons butter

**1.** Cook tortellini in lightly salted, boiling water for 4 minutes. Add the escarole and cook another 4 minutes. Drain.

**2.** Meanwhile, heat the oil over medium high in a nonstick skillet. Add the onions and garlic and cook 3 to 4 minutes, or until soft. Add the broth and wine, bring to a boil, and cook 2 to 3 minutes, or until slightly reduced.

**3.** Reduce heat to medium and stir in the tomatoes and cook 3 to 4 minutes. Add the butter and stir, cooking another 2 to 3 minutes, or until the sauce is thickened. Toss the sauce with the tortellini and escarole and serve in shallow bowls.

**Nutritional Analysis**
For each serving: 516 calories; 20 g. protein; 65 g. carbohydrates; 7 g. dietary fiber; 17 g. fat; 9 g. saturated fat; 58 mg. cholesterol, 641 mg. sodium.

**SERVING SUGGESTION**
Accompany with chick-pea and two tomato salad: Drain and rinse a can of chick-peas and toss with halved cherry tomatoes and finely chopped sun-dried tomatoes (look for sun-dried tomato bits sold similarly to bacon bits in wide shaker jars). Toss gently with a dressing of 1 tablespoon finely minced onion, 2 tablespoons balsamic vinegar, and 3 tablespoons extra-virgin olive oil. Season the salad with salt and pepper.

**SERVES 4**

# Tortilla Bean Stack

This is similar to a tostada, but I've replaced the more traditional corn tortillas with low-fat flour tortillas. In many ways, the dish is as good as the flavor of the salsa you buy, so splurge on a good one. I especially like green salsas, made from tomatillos. And if you have fresh cilantro on hand, toss a couple of tablespoons in between the layers for a more complex Mexican flavor.

## You Will Need

3 low-fat, burrito-sized flour tortillas
½ cup fat-free refried beans
4 tablespoons sour cream
1 (15-ounce) can kidney beans,
  drained and rinsed
1 (16-ounce) bottle chunky salsa
1 cup shredded light Cheddar cheese

**1.** Preheat the oven to 425 degrees.

**2.** Lay the tortillas out on a cookie sheet and coat lightly with cooking spray on both sides. Bake for 5 to 6 minutes, or until crisp and browned around the edges.

**3.** Place 1 tortilla in the bottom of a 9-inch pie plate. Coat with ¼ cup of the refried beans, 2 tablespoons of sour cream, ½ of the kidney beans, ½ of the salsa and ½ cup of the cheese.
Top with another tortilla and press down lightly with your palms.

**4.** Repeat the layers, finishing with 5 tablespoons of the shredded cheese. Place the final tortilla on top and sprinkle with the remaining 3 tablespoons of cheese. Bake for 15 to 20 minutes, or until heated through. Cut in wedges to serve.

### Nutritional Analysis
For each serving: 319 calories; 18 g. protein; 49 g. carbohydrates; 9 g. dietary fiber; 5 g. fat; 3 g. saturated fat; 11 mg. cholesterol, 1066 mg. sodium.

### SERVING SUGGESTION
Make a side dish of flash-sauteed vegetables: Heat olive oil in a large, nonstick skillet. Add finely minced garlic, thinly sliced carrots, broccoli, green beans and cauliflower (or any other bits and pieces of vegetables waiting in your crisper drawer) and saute, stirring, until brightly colored and crisp-tender. Toss with lime juice, lime zest and soy sauce.

**SHOPPING:**
Look for organic canned beans. They tend to have a firmer texture and less sodium than ordinary canned beans. Their taste is closer to that of home-cooked beans, although you'll still want to rinse them in a strainer under cold running water before using.

**SERVES 4**

# Vegetarian Chili

Most Americans think of chocolate as a dessert. In Mexico, however, chocolate is more commonly used in savory cooking, where it adds a depth of flavor to many dishes — and no sweetness. Many classic chilis include either cocoa or chocolate — or, as I've done here, a combination of the two. This savory and simple chili is as good on the buffet table as it is on a busy weeknight. And it doesn't taste like chocolate (much to the disappointment of my 11-year-old daughter Rachel who watched me make this).

## You Will Need

1 tablespoon canola oil
2 cloves garlic, minced
1 large onion, chopped
1 green pepper, chopped
1 (19-ounce) can kidney beans, drained and rinsed
1 (19-ounce) can black beans, drained and rinsed
1 (28-ounce) can whole plum tomatoes, chopped in their juices
1 tablespoon chili powder
1 tablespoon ground cumin
1 tablespoon cocoa powder
1 ounce semisweet chocolate, chopped
½ cup cilantro, chopped
1 teaspoon salt
½ teaspoon pepper
Tabasco sauce to taste

**1.** Heat the oil in a large pot over medium heat. Add garlic, onion and green pepper, and cook 3 to 4 minutes, or until softened. Add beans, tomatoes, chili powder, cumin and cocoa and bring to a boil. Immediately reduce heat and simmer 25 minutes, stirring occasionally.

**2.** Stir in chocolate, cilantro, salt and pepper, and Tabasco to taste. Serve immediately.

### Nutritional Analysis
For each serving: 413 calories; 21 g. protein; 69 g. carbohydrates; 24 g. dietary fiber; 9 g. fat; 2 g. saturated fat; 0 cholesterol, 1314 mg. sodium.

### SERVING SUGGESTIONS
Pass small bowls of chopped scallions and light sour cream that can be put on top of the chili.

Serve with baked tortilla chips and a salad of Romaine lettuce, croutons, tomato wedges topped with a low-fat dressing made by combining ¼ cup crumbled blue cheese with ½ cup low-fat buttermilk (or to desired consistency), a splash of vinegar and plenty of freshly ground black pepper.

**SERVES 4**

# Pizza & Sandwiches

*Indulge in a healthful version of an all-time favorite, Pizza with Sausage and Peppers.*

# Smoked Mozzarella and Chicken Pizza

## Good Idea

**SHOPPING:**

There are three convenience foods I use to make pizza on busy weeknights. The fastest is a prepared pizza crust, such as Boboli. You can also buy uncooked crust, sold in tubes, which has a nice, fresh-baked flavor. Best of all is the 1-pound bags of pizza dough sold in the refrigerated case of many supermarkets. Keep a spare at home in the freezer — the dough makes great pizza crusts, calzones and stuffed sandwiches.

Smoked mozzarella adds a wonderful depth of flavor to this pizza (I can't wait until a part-skim version becomes readily available). Many supermarkets sell smoked mozzarella in the refrigerated cheese case, but if yours doesn't, use regular part-skim. To get a smoky flavor, add a little crumbled bacon.

## You Will Need

1 pound refrigerated pizza dough
4 ounces smoked mozzarella, grated (about 1 cup)
¾ cup tomato pasta sauce
12 ounces cooked chicken, cut in chunks

**1.** Preheat the oven to 450 degrees. Coat a round pizza pan or a large baking sheet with cooking spray.

**2.** Stretch the dough into a 12-inch round or a large rectangle and place it on the baking sheet.

**3.** Stir half of the cheese into the pasta sauce and spread the mixture evenly over the dough, leaving a ½-inch border. Top with the chicken and sprinkle the remaining cheese over all. Bake for 20 minutes, or until the cheese is melted and the crust is golden. To serve, cut into 8 slices.

**Nutritional Analysis**
For each serving: 507 calories; 42 g. protein; 55 g. carbohydrates; 2.5 g. dietary fiber; 12.7 g. fat; 5.5 g. saturated fat; 95 mg. cholesterol, 1019 mg. sodium.

**SERVING SUGGESTIONS**
Accompany with quick bean soup: Combine drained and rinsed canned cannellini beans, chicken broth, chopped carrot, celery and onion and dried thyme in a saucepan and cook over medium heat until the vegetables are soft. Remove about half the mixture from the pot and puree it in a blender or food processor. Return the puree to the pot and mix well. Ladle soup into serving bowls and drizzle with extra-virgin olive oil.

Also, serve a salad of mixed greens dressed with an Italian vinaigrette made of 1 tablespoon red wine vinegar, 2 tablespoons extra-virgin olive oil, a dash of dried oregano and ½ teaspoon sugar.

**SERVES 4**

# Artichoke and Bacon Pizza

This pizza provides a great combination of flavors that is nothing like that of a typical pie with tomato sauce. If you happen to have Swiss or Jarlsberg cheese on hand, the flavor works beautifully in place of the mozzarella. Two slices of this pizza make a hearty serving that still gets less than 30 percent of its calories from fat. When served with a salad, this pizza makes an easy and well-balanced dinner.

## You Will Need

4 slices bacon
½ cup light ricotta cheese
1 (16-ounce) prepared pizza crust, such as Boboli
4 canned artichoke hearts, cut in quarters
½ cup shredded light mozzarella

**1.** Preheat the oven to 425 degrees.

**2.** Cook the bacon and let it cool on paper towels. Cut the bacon into 1-inch pieces.

**3.** Spread the ricotta over the surface of the pizza crust, leaving a ½-inch border all around. Arrange the bacon and quartered artichoke hearts in a random, but evenly dispersed pattern across the top of the pizza. Sprinkle with the shredded mozzarella. Place the pizza on the baking sheet and bake for 10 minutes, or until the cheese is melted and the pizza is warmed throughout. To serve, cut into 8 slices.

**Nutritional Analysis**
For each serving: 423 calories; 23 g. protein; 56 g. carbohydrates; 3 g. dietary fiber; 12 g. fat; 5 g. saturated fat; 15 mg. cholesterol, 866 mg. sodium.

**SERVING SUGGESTION**
Serve with a mixed green salad of thinly sliced radicchio, endive, arugula and Boston or Bibb lettuces. Add sliced radishes, rinsed canned white beans and halved grapes. Toss with orange-balsamic vinaigrette: 2 tablespoons orange juice, 1 tablespoon balsamic vinegar, 3 tablespoons extra-virgin olive oil, and salt and pepper to taste.

**SERVES 4**

# Sausage and Pepper Pizza

Pizza topped with slabs of mozzarella, as this one is, has a creamier texture than one made with the usual shredded cheese.

## You Will Need

¾ pound turkey sausage
1 onion, thinly sliced
½ red pepper, cut in strips
½ green pepper, cut in strips
1 (16-ounce) prepared pizza crust, such as Boboli
½ cup tomato pasta sauce
½ pound part-skim or light mozzarella, cut into ¼-inch slices, then into ½-inch strips

**1.** Preheat the oven to 425 degrees.

**2.** Squeeze the sausage out of its casing into a large skillet and cook over medium high for 4 minutes. Add the onions and peppers, and cook for 5 minutes.

**3.** Spread the surface of the pizza crust with the pasta sauce. Place the sliced mozzarella on top of the sauce. Top with the sausage and pepper mixture. Place the pizza on a baking sheet and bake for 10 minutes, or until the cheese is melted and bubbling around the edge. To serve, cut into 8 slices.

**Nutritional Analysis**
For each serving: 631 calories; 47 g. protein; 57 g. carbohydrates; 1.6 g. dietary fiber; 25.3 g. fat; 11.2 g. saturated fat; 101 mg. cholesterol, 1543 mg. sodium.

**SERVING SUGGESTION**
Accompany with cold tomato soup: Combine ½ cup parsley, 1 clove garlic and ½ small onion in the bowl of a food processor. Add 2 pounds quartered fresh tomatoes, ½ teaspoon dried thyme, ½ teaspoon dried basil, Tabasco to taste and 6 ice cubes and puree. Stir in 1 finely diced green pepper, 2 teaspoons red wine vinegar, and salt and pepper to taste. Let the soup sit 10 minutes before serving.

**SERVES 4**

# Greek Pizza

Feta, oregano and roasted peppers create a distinctively Greek-tasting pie that even died-in-the-wool fans of delivery pizza enjoy. You can make this pizza heartier simply by adding bite-size pieces of cooked chicken.

## You Will Need

1 tablespoon extra-virgin olive oil
1 onion, thinly sliced
1 teaspoon oregano
1 pound refrigerated pizza dough
¾ cup crumbled feta cheese
3 tablespoons grated Parmesan cheese
1 (7-ounce) jar roasted red peppers, drained and cut in thin strips
1 (15-ounce) can artichoke hearts, drained and cut in quarters

**1.** Preheat the oven to 450 degrees. Coat a round pizza pan or a large baking sheet with cooking spray.

**2.** Heat the oil in a skillet over medium high. Add the onions and oregano and cook for 7 minutes, stirring occasionally, until golden brown.

**3.** Stretch the dough into a 12-inch round or a large rectangle and place it on the baking sheet.

**4.** Sprinkle the dough with the feta and Parmesan, top with the onion and then the peppers and artichokes. Bake for 20 minutes, or until the crust is golden brown. To serve, cut into 8 slices.

### Nutritional Analysis
For each serving: 231 calories; 9 g. protein; 31 g. carbohydrates; 1.9 g. dietary fiber; 7.1 g. fat; 3.2 g. saturated fat; 14 mg. cholesterol, 696 mg. sodium.

### SERVING SUGGESTION
Serve with a salad of grapes, diced zucchini, green olives and fresh dill dressed with a lemon Dijon vinaigrette: Combine 2 tablespoons lemon juice, 1 tablespoon Dijon mustard, 2 tablespoons extra-virgin olive oil, 1 teaspoon honey, and salt and pepper to taste.

## Good Idea

**INGREDIENTS:**
Feta cheese keeps well in the refrigerator for a couple of weeks. It's a great boon for low-fat cooking, even though it is not low in fat. Because of feta's assertive flavor, a little goes a long way.

**SERVES 4**

# Pepperoni and Onion Pizza

I make sure to slice the pepperoni very thinly when I make this pizza, both because it's strongly flavored and because it's very high in fat. Some stores sell it pre-sliced in 4-ounce packages, which not only saves you work, but also means you don't have to buy too much of it.

## You Will Need

1 tablespoon olive oil
2 onions, thinly sliced
1 pound refrigerated pizza dough
½ cup prepared pizza-style tomato sauce
1½ cups shredded light mozzarella
2 ounces pepperoni, thinly sliced

**1.** Preheat the oven to 450 degrees. Coat a round pizza pan or a large baking sheet with cooking spray.

**2.** Heat the oil in a large skillet over medium high. Add the onions and cook, stirring occasionally, for 7 minutes, or until golden brown.

**3.** Stretch the pizza dough into a 12-inch round or a large rectangle and place on the baking sheet.

**4.** Spread the tomato sauce over the dough, leaving a ½-inch border all around. Sprinkle the cheese over the sauce and bake for 10 minutes. Top with the onions and pepperoni and bake 10 more minutes, or until the crust is golden brown. To serve, cut into 8 slices.

**Nutritional Analysis**
For each serving: 499 calories; 25 g. protein; 57 g. carbohydrates; 3.4 g. dietary fiber; 18.5 g. fat; 7.5 g. saturated fat; 28.8 mg. cholesterol, 1322 mg. sodium.

**SERVING SUGGESTION**
Accompany with zucchini boats: Cut 2 small zucchini in half lengthwise. Hollow out the centers with a melon scoop or spoon, reserving flesh. Place in a spoke pattern on a plate and microwave until just tender, about 3 minutes. Heat olive oil, add chopped onion, chopped prepared roasted red peppers and reserved zucchini flesh, and saute until tender, about 5 minutes. Stir in seasoned bread crumbs, grated Parmesan, and salt and pepper to taste. Fill zucchini shells with mixture and microwave again until shells are tender but hold their shape, about 2 more minutes.

**SERVES 4**

# Salad and Bean Pizza

Salad pizza is becoming increasingly popular, and with good reason. As odd as it may seem, the chewy crust, crunchy greens and creamy beans create an interesting combination of textures. It's also quite healthful, being a carbohydrate-based meatless meal.

## You Will Need

8 cups mixed salad greens, such as endive, radicchio, arugula and Boston lettuce
1 (15½-ounce) can cannellini beans, drained and rinsed
1 (7-ounce) jar roasted red peppers, drained and cut in ½-inch pieces
12 pitted kalamata olives, chopped
1 small red onion, thinly sliced
2 tablespoons extra-virgin olive oil
1 tablespoon balsamic vinegar
Salt and pepper to taste
1 (16-ounce) prepared pizza crust, such as Boboli
1 cup shredded light mozzarella

**1.** Preheat the oven to 425 degrees.

**2.** Cut the greens into 1-inch pieces. Lightly mash about half the beans with the back of a fork. Toss the greens and beans together and add the roasted peppers, olives, onion and remaining beans.

**3.** In a small bowl, combine the olive oil, balsamic vinegar, and salt and pepper to taste. Toss with the lettuce mixture.

**4.** Place the pizza crust on a baking sheet. Top it with the mozzarella and bake for 10 minutes. Gently press the greens and vegetables down onto the warm pizza with a spatula (to slightly compact the topping). Cut into 6 slices and serve immediately.

### Nutritional Analysis
For each serving: 399 calories; 17.6 g. protein; 50 g. carbohydrates; 5 g. dietary fiber; 13.5 g. fat; 4 g. saturated fat; 7 mg. cholesterol, 892 mg. sodium.

### SERVING SUGGESTION
Accompany with curried butternut soup: Peel a butternut squash and cut into 1-inch cubes. Boil until very tender and drain (to make a purely vegetarian version, reserve cooking liquid). Use an immersion blender, blender or food processor to puree the squash. Meanwhile, saute a finely chopped onion, minced fresh ginger and curry powder (2 to 3 teaspoons) in olive oil. Add the puree and chicken broth (or reserved cooking liquid) and cook 5 to 10 minutes, adding salt and pepper to taste.

## Good Idea

**COOKING:**
Immersion blenders make easy work of homemade soups. You can plug in this small, relatively inexpensive appliance near the stove. Cook your vegetables in flavored broth, and when they're soft, place the immersion blender in the pot to puree the vegetables.

**SERVES 6**

# Chicken and Broccoli Calzones

Refrigerated pizza dough is sticky and elastic, but it is also forgiving. After using it once, you'll be a pro at it. Don't worry if your calzones look a little rough as they go into the oven; you'll be impressed with the finished product 20 minutes later. You will use only about half of a 10-ounce box of frozen chopped broccoli in this recipe, so save the leftovers to use in a salad or a stir-fry another night.

## You Will Need

1 cup frozen chopped broccoli
1 pound refrigerated pizza dough
10 ounces cooked chicken, diced
 (about 2 cups)
1 cup shredded light mozzarella
1 egg, lightly beaten

**1.** Preheat the oven to 450 degrees. Coat a baking sheet with cooking spray.

**2.** Cook the broccoli according to package instructions, and then drain in a colander or strainer.

**3.** Cut the dough in 4 pieces. Lightly flour the work surface and your hands and pull one piece of the dough into a rectangle measuring 7 inches by 6 inches. Lay ¼ of the chicken on half the rectangle, leaving a ½-inch border. Place ¼ cup of the broccoli and ¼ cup of the cheese on the chicken. Fold the dough over and seal the edges by rolling the bottom edge slightly up over the top edge and then pressing it with the tines of a fork. Poke holes in the top of the calzone to allow steam to escape. Transfer to the baking sheet and brush lightly with the egg. Repeat with the remaining ingredients. Bake for 20 minutes, or until lightly browned, then serve.

### Nutritional Analysis
For each serving: 519 calories; 44 g. protein; 52 g. carbohydrates; 3.7 g. dietary fiber; 14.5 g. fat; 5.5 g. saturated fat; 129 mg. cholesterol, 861 mg. sodium.

### SERVING SUGGESTIONS
Serve with carrots and dip: Blanch or microwave baby carrots, and serve with a dip made from light sour cream mixed with lemon juice, dried oregano and thyme.
  Also, serve a salad of mixed greens dressed with an Italian vinaigrette made of 1 tablespoon red wine vinegar, 2 tablespoons extra-virgin olive oil, a dash of dried oregano and ½ teaspoon sugar.

**SERVES 4**

# Sausage Eppie Roll

A cross between a pig-in-a-blanket and a calzone, this seemingly sinful roll encases sausage, cheese and vegetables. This is one of those dinners that looks like you went to great effort, but takes only 10 minutes to prepare (another 25 minutes to bake, unattended). And it is ideal for casual entertaining (the roll can even be sliced and served as a starter).

## You Will Need

1 pound refrigerated bread dough
1 cup shredded light mozzarella
4 (3-ounce) precooked chicken sausages (preferably artichoke and roasted garlic flavored)
1 (13¾-ounce) can quartered artichokes, drained
1 (7-ounce) jar roasted red peppers, drained, rinsed and patted dry

**1.** Preheat the oven to 400 degrees. Coat a baking sheet with cooking spray.

**2.** Cut the dough in 4 pieces. Working on a lightly floured surface, roll 1 piece of dough into a 7-inch circle. Sprinkle ¼ cup of the cheese in a strip down the center, leaving a 1-inch border at the top and bottom. Place a sausage on top of the cheese. Place ¼ of the artichokes along one side of the sausage and ¼ of the peppers along the other side. Fold the sides of the dough up toward the center, overlapping them by about 2 inches. Repeat with the remaining ingredients, using a spatula to transfer the rolls to the baking sheet. Bake for 25 minutes, or until the rolls are lightly browned. Tap the bread lightly with your fingertips: it should feel solid and sound somewhat hollow. Let the rolls cool slightly before serving.

**Nutritional Analysis**
For each serving: 534 calories; 34 g. protein; 60.1 g. carbohydrates; 7.2 g. dietary fiber; 16 g. fat; 6.2 g. saturated fat; 86 mg. cholesterol, 1633 mg. sodium.

**SERVING SUGGESTION**
Accompany with mustard-dressed broccoli rabe: Boil rabe until bright green and fork tender (do not overcook to the point where the color starts to dull). Drain, then saute in olive oil with minced garlic and toss with country-style Dijon mustard.

**SERVES 4**

# Turkey, Ham and Cheese Filled Bread

Think of this as a hot sandwich in freshly baked bread. I keep bags of pizza dough in my freezer (move it to the refrigerator in the morning to thaw it in time for dinner), and always find some great combination of ingredients in my pantry and refrigerator to make it into a full-fledged dinner.

To cut back on the sodium, simply substitute the low-sodium deli meats now available at almost all supermarkets. And if you want to cut back on fat and calories, use all turkey and no ham.

## You Will Need

1 pound refrigerated pizza dough
½ pound sliced turkey
3 tablespoons diced sun-dried tomatoes
2 cups arugula
½ pound sliced ham
1½ cups shredded light mozzarella
1 (14-ounce) jar roasted red peppers, drained and patted dry
1 egg, lightly beaten

**1.** Preheat the oven to 400 degrees and lightly coat a baking sheet or jelly-roll pan with cooking spray.

**2.** Working on a lightly floured work surface, stretch or roll pizza dough into a 12-by-8-inch rectangle. Leaving a 1-inch border, lay the turkey slices over the dough. Sprinkle with the sun-dried tomatoes, then top with a layer of the arugula, then the ham, then the mozzarella and finally the roasted peppers. Fold the bread lengthwise in thirds, overlapping the edges by about two inches, then pinching the dough at the seam lightly to seal it.

**3.** Brush the top of the sandwich lightly with beaten egg and bake for about 35 minutes, or until lightly browned. Tap the bread lightly with your fingertips: it should feel solid and sound somewhat hollow. Let the sandwich cool slightly before cutting it into 4 pieces and serving.

**Nutritional Analysis**
For each serving: 596 calories; 43 g. protein; 63 g. carbohydrates; 3.8 g. dietary fiber; 16.2 g. fat; 7.3 g. saturated fat; 70 mg. cholesterol, 2606 mg. sodium.

**SERVING SUGGESTION**
Accompany with a green salad with chopped celery, grated carrot, green beans, cherry tomatoes, cucumber and any leftover cooked vegetables. Dress with a light red wine vinaigrette: 1 to 2 tablespoons red wine vinegar, 3 tablespoons extra-virgin olive oil, a pinch of sugar or to taste, and salt and pepper to taste.

**SERVES 4**

# Sloppy Joes with Corn

Sloppy Joes are like corn on the cob and ice cream sandwiches — part of the fun is devising your personal technique for eating them. My kids and I like to let the sauce from this version — one of several Sloppy Joes I make regularly — soak into the bun, which we save for last, after downing the filling with a fork. This filling also makes great pasta sauce.

## You Will Need

1 teaspoon oil
1 onion, chopped
2 cloves garlic, minced
1 green pepper, diced
1 pound lean (93 percent fat-free)
    ground turkey
1 teaspoon chili powder
½ teaspoon dry mustard
½ teaspoon salt
⅛ teaspoon pepper, or to taste
1 cup frozen corn
1 (15-ounce) can crushed tomatoes
2 teaspoons molasses
6 hamburger buns, toasted

**1.** Heat the oil in a large skillet over medium high. Add the onion, garlic and green pepper, and cook for 3 minutes or until soft. Add the turkey, chili powder, dry mustard, salt and pepper, and cook, stirring, for 4 minutes. Stir in the corn, tomatoes and molasses, and cook, stirring occasionally, for 5 more minutes, or until slightly thickened. Serve on the hamburger buns.

### Nutritional Analysis
For each serving: 308 calories; 22 g. protein; 38 g. carbohydrates; 4.3 g. dietary fiber; 8.9 g. fat; 2 g. saturated fat; 47 mg. cholesterol, 590 mg. sodium.

### SERVING SUGGESTION
Accompany with cucumber-watercress salad: Combine ½ cup plain nonfat yogurt, 1 teaspoon lemon juice, salt, pepper and a dash of Tabasco. Grate a cucumber and squeeze out excess moisture. Add to yogurt mixture along with ½ cup finely chopped red onion and 1 bunch watercress.

**SERVES 6**

# Turkey and Black Bean Sloppy Joes

Black beans seem to have a meaty, almost smoky flavor compared with other beans. They add depth and a creamy texture to the traditional Sloppy Joe — as well as fiber and other nutrients.

## You Will Need

1 teaspoon oil
1 onion, chopped
1 clove garlic, minced
½ green pepper, chopped
1 pound lean (93 percent fat-free) ground turkey
1 (14½-ounce) can diced tomatoes
¼ cup tomato paste
1 tablespoon spicy brown mustard
2 teaspoons chili powder
1 teaspoon cumin
½ teaspoon salt
¼ teaspoon pepper
1 (15-ounce) can black beans, drained and rinsed
6 hamburger buns
1 cup shredded light Cheddar cheese

**1.** Heat the oil in a large skillet over medium high. Add the onion, garlic and green pepper, and cook for 2 minutes. Add the turkey, diced tomatoes, tomato paste, mustard, chili powder, cumin, salt and pepper and cook, stirring, for 1 to 2 minutes as the mixture comes to a boil.

**2.** Cover, reduce the heat and simmer for 10 minutes. Stir in the black beans and cook 2 more minutes, or until the beans are warmed through. Spoon the mixture onto the buns, top with the Cheddar cheese, close the sandwiches and serve immediately.

Note: To melt the cheese, put the sandwiches under the broiler or top the buns with the cheese and heat them in the oven so the cheese melts right onto the bread.

**Nutritional Analysis**
For each serving: 363 calories; 29 g. protein; 38 g. carbohydrates; 6.5 g. dietary fiber; 11.6 g. fat; 3.1 g. saturated fat; 52 mg. cholesterol, 951 mg. sodium.

**SERVING SUGGESTION**
Accompany with braised fennel: Cut 2 fennel bulbs in half lengthwise, remove cores and slice thinly. Heat 1 tablespoon olive oil in a large skillet, add fennel and cook 2 minutes. Add 1 cup nonfat chicken broth, salt and pepper, bring to a boil, reduce heat and simmer until fennel is soft.

**SERVES 6**

# Stuffed Buns

can talk about Popeye and muscles until I'm blue in the face, and my eight-year-old son still won't touch spinach (or any other leafy green). This dish, however, he'll eat, despite the presence of the ominous green monster. What's more, my daughter loves to take any leftover buns to school for lunch — they're great cold. Any leftover filling can be used as a pasta sauce or to make a Sloppy Joe-type sandwich. When you bake these buns, they may leak slightly, but don't worry if the bottoms get dark brown — they will not burn (even if the leaked liquid does).

## You Will Need

½ pound lean (93 percent fat-free) ground turkey
½ onion, chopped
1 (10-ounce) box frozen spinach
½ cup nonfat chicken broth
½ cup tomato sauce
1 tablespoon red wine vinegar
2 (7½-ounce) tubes refrigerated country biscuits

**1.** Preheat the oven to 450 degrees and coat a jelly-roll pan with cooking spray.

**2.** Combine the turkey and onion in a nonstick skillet and cook over medium high for 5 minutes, stirring occasionally. Add the frozen spinach, chicken broth, tomato sauce and vinegar, cover, and cook 5 more minutes, breaking up the spinach with a fork.

**3.** To assemble the buns, place one biscuit directly on top of another on the baking sheet. Press the two biscuits down firmly with the heel of your hand and pull the edges out to form a 5-inch circle. Place ¼ cup of the turkey mixture in the center of the dough, then fold the sides up toward the center (like pleats) overlapping them, as though forming a beggar's purse. Turn the filled bun seam side down and repeat with the remaining biscuits to make 10 buns. Bake for 10 minutes, or until golden brown. Let cool slightly before serving.

**Nutritional Analysis**
For each serving: 310 calories; 18 g. protein; 47 g. carbohydrates; 4 g. dietary fiber; 6.7 g. fat; 1.5 g. saturated fat; 28 mg. cholesterol, 911 mg. sodium.

**SERVING SUGGESTION**
Accompany with linguine with artichokes: Cook linguine until al dente according to package instructions. Cook 1 box frozen artichokes according to package instructions. Toss the linguine and artichokes with olive oil and Parmesan cheese.

**SERVES 5**

# Ham and Cheddar Biscuits

## DESSERT:

Fresh or frozen blueberries can be used to make a delicious dessert sauce. Combine 1 cup whole berries with ½ cup water and ¼ cup sugar in a saucepan. Bring to a boil, then simmer until thickened, about 12 minutes. Remove from heat and stir in 1 cup berries. Serve over low-fat frozen yogurt, ice cream or angel food cake.

These sandwiches are a lower-fat version of the Southern ham and cheese biscuit that is eaten for both breakfast and lunch. Low-fat cheese doesn't melt the way regular cheese does, but when combined with the sour cream, it becomes soft and creamy and makes this sandwich taste devilishly rich. When served as suggested with a bowl of slightly spicy Tex-Mex tomato soup, these biscuits make a perfect light supper. Be sure to pass the bottle of Tabasco at the table for people who like their soup fiery.

## You Will Need

1 tube oversized reduced-fat refrigerated biscuits
1 tablespoon Dijon mustard
6 ounces sliced low-fat smoked ham
½ cup shredded light Cheddar cheese
2 tablespoons light sour cream
1 tomato, sliced
4 teaspoons pickle relish

**1.** Bake the biscuits according to package instructions. Split 4 of them horizontally and spread the bottom half of each with the mustard. (Reserve the remaining baked biscuits for breakfast or to use for sandwiches.) Divide the ham evenly among the biscuits and place on top of the mustard.

**2.** Mix the Cheddar cheese into the sour cream. Divide the mixture evenly among the biscuits and spread on top of the ham. Place in the warm oven for 5 minutes, or until the cheese is heated through. Top each with a tomato slice, 1 teaspoon relish and the other biscuit half, and serve immediately.

**Nutritional Analysis**
For each serving: 268 calories; 15 g. protein; 31 g. carbohydrates; 1 g. dietary fiber; 9 g. fat; 3 g. saturated fat; 21 mg. cholesterol, 1195 mg. sodium.

**SERVING SUGGESTION**
Serve with Tex-Mex tomato soup: In a saucepan, combine 2 (15-ounce) cans chunky chile tomato sauce, 2 cups nonfat chicken broth, 1 cup frozen corn, ⅛ teaspoon Tabasco, and salt and pepper to taste. Simmer for 10 minutes.

**SERVES 4**

# Roast Beef and Creamy Horseradish Wraps

Although the recipe says this serves four, you may find you get as many as eight servings from it — depending on the appetite of your family members. These are large wraps. If you think you'll have leftovers, go a little light on the dressing so the wraps won't get soggy if refrigerated overnight.

## You Will Need

2 tablespoons prepared horseradish
½ cup light mayonnaise
½ cup light sour cream
4 low-fat, burrito-sized flour tortillas
1 pound deli roast beef
6 leaves lettuce, core removed
2 beefsteak tomatoes, thinly sliced

**1.** Combine the horseradish, mayonnaise and sour cream in a bowl.

**2.** Working with 1 wrap at a time, lay a tortilla on your work surface. Spread it with about ¼ cup of the horseradish mixture, leaving a 1-inch border all around. Top with ¼ pound of the roast beef and a layer of lettuce. Cover half the surface with ¼ of the tomato slices. Roll the sandwich as tightly as possible and wrap with plastic wrap or foil. Refrigerate 10 minutes, cut each sandwich in half, and serve.

### Nutritional Analysis
For each serving: 440 calories; 29 g. protein; 37 g. carbohydrates; 2.5 g. dietary fiber; 19.7 g. fat; 5.7 g. saturated fat; 65 mg. cholesterol, 1647 mg. sodium.

### SERVING SUGGESTION
Serve with a chopped salad: Cut iceberg lettuce, radishes, cucumber, carrots and any other crunchy vegetables into ¾-inch pieces. Add drained and rinsed chick-peas and bits of orange or melon. Toss with an Italian vinaigrette made of 1 tablespoon red wine vinegar, 2 tablespoons extra-virgin olive oil, a dash of dried oregano and ½ teaspoon sugar.

**SERVES 4**

# Chicken Quesadillas

You can make the filling for these quesadillas and keep it warm while you prepare the rest of the meal. But don't grill the tortillas and assemble the quesadillas until right before serving so they'll be crunchy.

## You Will Need

1 teaspoon canola oil
1 cup chopped red onion
1 green pepper, thinly sliced
1½ cups prepared salsa
10 ounces cooked chicken, diced (about 2 cups)
4 low-fat, burrito-sized flour tortillas
2 cups shredded light Cheddar cheese

**1.** Heat the oil over medium high in a skillet. Add the onion and pepper and cook, stirring occasionally, for 5 minutes or until soft. Add the salsa and chicken, reduce the heat to medium, and simmer for 5 minutes.

**2.** Heat a second skillet (don't put any oil in it) over medium high. Add one tortilla and cook 15 to 30 seconds, or until browned on the underside. Sprinkle with ½ cup of cheese, and place ¼ of the chicken mixture over the half of the tortilla farthest from the pan's handle. Immediately fold the tortilla over, omelet style, and press down lightly with your spatula for 10 seconds. Slide the quesadilla onto a dinner plate and repeat the procedure with the remaining ingredients. Cut in half to serve.

### Nutritional Analysis
For each serving: 446 calories; 41 g. protein; 40 g. carbohydrates; 3 g. dietary fiber; 14 g. fat; 5 g. saturated fat; 71 mg. cholesterol, 1159 mg. sodium.

### SERVING SUGGESTION
Serve with carrot and jicama salad: Peel jicama and grate on the large holes of a box grater (or in the food processor). Combine with a bag of shredded carrots, raisins, a pinch of cumin, salt, pepper, canola oil and apple cider vinegar.

**SERVES 4**

# Chicken Sandwiches with Blue Cheese and Barbecue Sauce

Inspired by the flavors of Buffalo chicken wings with blue cheese dip, this sandwich tastes every bit as decadent — but gets fewer than 30 percent of its calories from fat. It can be made using leftover or store-bought chicken cut in large pieces.

## You Will Need

½ cup crumbled blue cheese, about 2 ounces
¼ cup light mayonnaise
¼ cup plain nonfat yogurt
2 teaspoons apple cider vinegar
½ teaspoon Worcestershire sauce
4 (4-ounce) boneless chicken breasts
4 hard rolls, cut in half horizontally
4 large leaves romaine lettuce
½ cup bottled smoke-flavored (such as hickory or mesquite) barbecue sauce

**1.** Combine the blue cheese, mayonnaise, yogurt, vinegar and Worcestershire sauce in a bowl and set aside.

**2.** Coat a grill pan or broiler pan with cooking spray and heat. Grill or broil chicken for 4 to 5 minutes on each side, or until cooked through.

**3.** Spread the blue cheese dressing evenly over the bottom half of each roll. Top each with the lettuce and chicken. Spread the top half of each roll with the barbecue sauce. Close the sandwich and serve.

**Nutritional Analysis**
For each serving: 450 calories; 36.3 g. protein; 43 g. carbohydrates; 1.3 g. dietary fiber; 13.7 g. fat; 4.9 g. saturated fat; 79 mg. cholesterol, 1188 mg. sodium.

**SERVING SUGGESTION**
Accompany with "instant" slaw: Peel 2 carrots, shred in a food processor or grate on the large holes of a box grater. Cut ½ of a small head Savoy cabbage into thin strips. Toss carrots and cabbage with 2 to 3 tablespoons apple cider vinegar, 2 to 3 teaspoons sugar, ½ teaspoon fennel seeds, and salt and pepper to taste.

**SERVES 4**

# Portobello, Fontina and Tomato Sandwiches

**INGREDIENTS:**
When making a stir-fry or stew, try substituting portobellos for one-fourth of the meat called for in the recipe. They're easy to clean: simply wipe the caps off with a damp paper towel. To store portobellos for several days, keep them in a paper bag in the refrigerator.

This is a meaty and sophisticated vegetarian substitute for the all-American burger. Portobello mushrooms have a deep, earthy flavor that can be used both in combination with and instead of meat in many recipes.

## You Will Need
1 teaspoon balsamic vinegar
4 teaspoons extra-virgin olive oil
1 teaspoon dried rosemary
½ teaspoon salt
4 large portobello caps, wiped clean
4 ounces sharp fontina cheese
4 English muffins or other hard rolls
2 beefsteak tomatoes, thinly sliced

**1.** Combine the vinegar, oil, rosemary and salt in a small bowl, and whisk thoroughly. Pour the mixture over the gill side of the mushroom caps and let sit for 10 minutes.

**2.** Meanwhile, cut the cheese in thin strips. Cut the muffins in half and toast.

**3.** Heat a nonstick skillet over medium heat. Add the mushrooms gill side down and cook for 5 minutes, turn and cook 3 more minutes. Distribute the cheese evenly among the caps, cover the pan and cook 2 more minutes or until the cheese is melted. Divide the mushrooms and tomato slices among the muffins. Close the sandwiches and serve.

**Nutritional Analysis**
For each serving: 340 calories; 18.2 g. protein; 38 g. carbohydrates; 8.3 g. dietary fiber; 14.8 g. fat; 6.3 g. saturated fat; 33 mg. cholesterol, 808 mg. sodium.

**SERVING SUGGESTION**
Serve with a romaine salad tossed with drained and rinsed canned chick-peas, tomato wedges, thinly sliced red onion and grapes. Dress with a balsamic vinaigrette: 1 to 2 tablespoons balsamic vinegar, 3 tablespoons extra-virgin olive oil, a pinch of sugar or to taste, and salt and pepper to taste.

**SERVES 4**

# Turkey and Ham Muffuletta

This sandwich, beloved in New Orleans, is traditionally made by filling a hollowed-out loaf of bread with olive salad and high-fat cold cuts. This more healthful version uses sliced deli turkey and low-fat deli ham.

## You Will Need

2 (7-ounce) jars green salad olives, drained and chopped
1 teaspoon oregano
2 tablespoons lemon juice
¼ teaspoon pepper
1 tablespoon red wine vinegar
1 (1½-pound) round white bread, such as a boule
2 romaine lettuce leaves
¾ pound sliced deli turkey
6 ounces sliced deli low-fat ham
1 (12-ounce) jar roasted red peppers, drained

**1.** Combine the olives, oregano, lemon juice, pepper and vinegar in a bowl and set aside.

**2.** Cut the bread in half horizontally. Hollow out the inside (top and bottom) by pulling the soft bread out with your fingers, leaving a 1-inch border all around.

**3.** Spread half of the olive mixture in the bottom piece of bread and cover with a layer of lettuce. Top with half the turkey, half the ham and then all the roasted peppers. Layer the rest of the turkey on top, followed by the remaining ham and the olive mixture.

**4.** Replace the top half of the bread. Wrap the filled loaf with plastic wrap. Place a baking sheet on top of the sandwich and weight it with a couple of large cans. Press the sandwich for at least 20 minutes (or overnight — the flavors just get better as the olive salad juices soak into the bread). Unwrap and cut into 6 wedges to serve.

### Nutritional Analysis
For each serving: 544 calories; 28 g. protein; 67 g. carbohydrates; 4 g. dietary fiber; 15 g. fat; 1 g. saturated fat; 35 mg. cholesterol, 2993 mg. sodium.

### SERVING SUGGESTION
Accompany with cooked tomato and zucchini salad: Cut zucchini in quarters lengthwise, then across in slices. Cut cherry tomatoes in half. Heat olive oil in a skillet over medium, add garlic and cook 1 minute. Add vegetables and cook, stirring often, until zucchini is just tender, about 5 minutes. Add salt and pepper to taste.

**SERVES 6**

# Good Enough for Guests

*A savory mixture of spinach and rice completes Flank Steak Roulade.*

# Chicken Breasts Stuffed with Ham and Cheese

### COOKING:

Don't underestimate the power of a garnish. Simply adding a mint leaf or a parsley sprig to your dish can give it a polished look. Instead of grating Parmesan on top of pasta or a salad, buy a block of cheese and use a vegetable peeler to create giant, dramatic Parmesan curls. Also, fresh fruit can really dress up a plate. Add a slice of melon, an orange wedge or a few grapes to add color and panache.

Based on the classic chicken cordon bleu, this simple dinner uses low-fat sliced deli ham and part-skim Jarlsberg cheese to make it more healthful than the traditional version. However, if you splurge and use slightly higher fat prosciutto, the flavor is incomparable. Most of the fat in this dish comes from the chicken skin, which must be left on. If you're watching your weight or fat intake, bake the chicken as instructed, then remove the skin before serving.

## You Will Need

1 tablespoon Dijon mustard
¾ teaspoon caraway seeds
4 bone-in chicken breasts,
    about 2½ pounds
2 ounces sliced low-fat ham
2 ounces sliced Jarlsberg cheese
⅛ teaspoon pepper

**1.** Preheat the oven to 425 degrees.

**2.** Combine the mustard and caraway seeds in a small bowl.

**3.** Lift the skin from each breast without completely detaching it, and spread the mustard mixture evenly over the surface of the chicken flesh. Place 1 slice each of ham and cheese over the mustard, and cover by folding the skin back into place. Sprinkle the breasts with the pepper. Bake for 35 to 40 minutes, or until an instant-read thermometer registers 160 degrees when inserted into the thickest part of the breast (without touching the bone). Serve immediately.

**Nutritional Analysis**

For each serving: 322 calories; 37 g. protein; 1.2 g. carbohydrates; <1 g. dietary fiber; 18 g. fat; 6.6 g. saturated fat; 110 mg. cholesterol, 423 mg. sodium.

**SERVING SUGGESTIONS**

Serve with broad egg noodles cooked according to package instructions, then tossed with a sauce made of grated Parmesan cheese, light sour cream, a dash of nutmeg, and salt and pepper to taste.

Also, serve peas and pearl onions tossed with balsamic vinegar, salt and pepper.

For a salad, combine fresh spinach with orange segments and thinly sliced red onion. Dress with a vinaigrette made from 1 tablespoon fresh orange juice, 1 tablespoon balsamic vinegar, 4 tablespoons extra-virgin olive oil, and salt, pepper and thyme to taste.

**SERVES 4**

# Golden Chicken with Grapes and Almonds

This is an elegant-looking dish. Thin-sliced, boneless chicken breasts are sauteed to a lovely golden brown in less than 5 minutes.

I prepare this dish in a 12-inch, nonstick skillet, which allows me to cook all the chicken at once. If you only have a smaller pan, you may have to saute the chicken in 2 batches.

## You Will Need

1 pound thin-sliced boneless
  chicken breasts
½ teaspoon salt
⅛ teaspoon pepper
2 teaspoons olive oil
½ cup nonfat chicken broth
2 tablespoons balsamic vinegar
1 cup green seedless grapes
  (or mixed green and red grapes)
¼ cup sliced almonds

**1.** Sprinkle the chicken with the salt and pepper. In a large, nonstick skillet, heat the oil over medium high. Add the chicken and cook about 1½ minutes on each side, or until golden brown. (You'll know when to turn them because the top edges become opaque.) Transfer the chicken to a plate.

**2.** Add the broth, vinegar and grapes to the skillet, and cook for 3 minutes. (The grapes will just start to split and the liquid will reduce and thicken slightly.)

**3.** Return the chicken to the skillet. Spoon the grapes and sauce on top of the chicken. Sprinkle with the almonds, cover and cook for 2 minutes. Serve immediately.

**Nutritional Analysis**
For each serving: 214 calories; 28 g. protein; 10 g. carbohydrates; 1 g. dietary fiber; 6.9 g. fat; 1 g. saturated fat; 66 mg. cholesterol, 447 mg. sodium.

**SERVING SUGGESTIONS**
Accompany with peppery orange couscous: Heat 1 teaspoon extra-virgin olive oil, add 1 minced garlic clove, ½ cup chopped onion and ¼ teaspoon black pepper (or to taste), and cook 2 minutes. Add ¾ cup orange juice and ½ cup water or chicken broth, and bring to a boil. Remove from heat, add 1 cup couscous, cover and let stand 15 minutes. Stir in chopped parsley.

Also, steam broccoli and toss it with bottled chopped pimientos, extra-virgin olive oil, marjoram and red wine vinegar.

**SERVES 4**

# Flank Steak Roulade

A simple flank steak is given panache when lightly pounded, filled with a savory stuffing and rolled. The resulting slices are as delicious as they are attractive.

## You Will Need

1 cup quick-cooking brown rice
4 scallions, chopped (about ½ cup)
1 (10-ounce) box frozen spinach, thawed and squeezed dry
⅛ teaspoon nutmeg
1 to 1¼ pounds flank steak
½ cup shredded light mozzarella
1 teaspoon paprika
½ teaspoon salt
¼ teaspoon pepper

**1.** Preheat the oven to 450 degrees. Coat a baking dish with cooking spray.

**2.** Cook the rice according to package instructions. Stir in the scallions, spinach and nutmeg, and set aside to cool.

**3.** Meanwhile, place the flank steak on a piece of plastic wrap. Cover with another piece of plastic and pound to an even ½-inch thickness.

**4.** Stir the cheese into the cooled rice and place about 1½ cups of the rice mixture in the center of the meat. Roll the meat jellyroll-style, enclosing the rice mixture. Tie with kitchen string. Combine the paprika, salt and pepper in a small bowl and sprinkle the mixture over the entire surface of the meat.

**5.** Place the meat in the dish and spoon the remaining rice around it. Roast for 30 minutes. (If the rice begins to dry out, sprinkle 2 tablespoons of water over the top.) Remove from the oven and let it sit for 5 minutes. Cut across on a diagonal into 1-inch-thick slices. Place the slices on top of the extra rice to serve.

**Nutritional Analysis**

For each serving: 367 calories; 38 g. protein; 21 g. carbohydrates; 4 g. dietary fiber; 14 g. fat; 6 g. saturated fat; 78 mg. cholesterol, 540 mg. sodium.

**SERVING SUGGESTION**

Accompany with roasted tomatoes and onions: Place wedges of plum tomatoes and sliced red onion in a roasting pan, toss with olive oil, salt and pepper and roast in a 450-degree oven until onions are soft, stirring occasionally.

**SERVES 4**

# Fig-stuffed Pork Loin Roast

You can substitute other dried fruits, such as apricots and raisins, for the figs and cranberries in this recipe. No matter what you put in the center, the roast looks quite impressive when you slice it. More importantly, it has a rich, slightly sweet flavor that makes this recipe a winner whether you're serving it on a busy weeknight to family or on a special occasion to company.

## You Will Need

6 dried black mission figs
2 tablespoons dried cranberries
1 piece crystallized ginger, chopped
¼ teaspoon ground ginger
2 tablespoons Marsala wine
1 pound lean pork loin roast
½ teaspoon salt
Black pepper to taste

**1.** Preheat the oven to 425 degrees. Coat a baking dish with cooking spray.

**2.** Combine the figs, cranberries, crystallized ginger, ground ginger and Marsala wine in a bowl and set aside.

**3.** Cut the pork loin lengthwise so you can open it as you would a book. Place the figs on one half of the roast in a single layer and top with the cranberries and pieces of ginger. Pour a small amount of the liquid over the figs. Close the roast back up and tie it with kitchen string overlapping the meat slightly, if possible.

**4.** Place the roast in the baking dish, sprinkle with the salt and pepper, and pour the remaining Marsala mixture over the top. Roast for about 40 minutes, or until cooked to an internal temperature of 155 degrees. Let the roast rest for 5 minutes before slicing. (The temperature will increase about 5 degrees.)

**Nutritional Analysis**
For each serving: 316 calories; 24 g. protein; 23 g. carbohydrates; 4 g. dietary fiber; 13 g. fat; 5 g. saturated fat; 70 mg. cholesterol, 346 mg. sodium.

**SERVING SUGGESTIONS**
Serve with mashed parsnip-potatoes: Cut parsnips into ¼-inch-thick slices and potatoes into ½-inch dice. Boil together until tender. Drain and combine with skim milk, butter, salt and pepper and mash.
   Also, serve cooked baby-cut carrots tossed with a pinch of Chinese five-spice powder and sesame oil.

**SERVES 4**

# Stuffed Pork Cutlets

**FREEZER:**

If you buy a larger piece of meat than your recipe calls for, cut the leftover portion into cutlets, steaks or even stir-fry strips and then freeze. The smaller cuts of meat will defrost more quickly than a whole roast and some of your prep work will already be done. For example, pork tenderloins are usually sold in packages of two: Cut the second into medallions or strips before freezing.

Tenderloin is the leanest cut of pork there is, and it is ideally suited to grilling and roasting. But don't just use it as a roast, the tenderloins can easily be made into versatile and quick-cooking "cutlets." Simply lay the tenderloin out on a work surface. Cut across it at an extremely sharp diagonal to make four even pieces. The sharper the diagonal, the more even your cutlets will end up. Take each of the four pieces and, starting at the center, gently pound out each one until it's about ¼ inch thick.

## You Will Need

1 pound pork tenderloin, cut in 4 pieces and pounded to ¼ inch thickness
1 tablespoon kalamata olive spread
1 (7-ounce) jar roasted red peppers, drained
¼ cup shredded light mozzarella
1 tablespoon grated Parmesan cheese

**1.** Preheat the oven to 450 degrees.

**2.** Lay the cutlets out on a work surface. Spread a thin layer of kalamata paste over them. Then lay the roasted red peppers on top, leaving a 1-inch border around the edges of each cutlet. Top the peppers with the mozzarella, then roll the cutlets up as tightly as possible.

**3.** Place the stuffed pork rolls seam side down in a baking dish and sprinkle with the Parmesan. Bake for 30 minutes, or until cooked through. Serve immediately.

**Nutritional Analysis**
For each serving: 193 calories; 26.6 g. protein; 1.8 g. carbohydrates; <1 g. dietary fiber; 6.6 g. fat; 2.3 g. saturated fat; 71 mg. cholesterol, 330 mg. sodium.

**SERVING SUGGESTIONS**
Accompany with steamed green beans tossed with sliced almonds, salt, pepper and olive oil.
Also, saute finely diced red pepper, onion, garlic and thyme. Toss with basmati rice and fresh chopped parsley.

**SERVES 4**

# Coconut Shrimp Soup

The flavors of this soup come from Thailand, but the ingredients come from your neighborhood supermarket. This is an impressively exotic dinner that couldn't be any easier to make. If you've never used fish sauce before, you may be surprised when you first open the bottle. It always baffles me that something that smells so unpleasant can make food taste so good. Once opened, keep the bottle in the refrigerator, where it will last for a year or so.

## You Will Need

¾ cup jasmine rice
1 pound peeled shrimp, shells reserved
6 cups (1 [48-ounce] can) nonfat chicken broth
¼ cup fresh lime juice
3 tablespoons Asian fish sauce
1 (½-inch) piece fresh ginger, peeled and cut in thin slices
¼ teaspoon red pepper flakes, or to taste
1 tablespoon brown sugar
1 (15-ounce) can straw mushrooms
1 cup light coconut milk
1 teaspoon lime zest

**1.** Cook the rice according to package instructions.

**2.** Coat the bottom of a saucepan with cooking spray and heat over medium high. Add the shrimp shells and cook, stirring, for 1 minute. Add the broth, bring to a boil, reduce heat and simmer for 5 minutes. Remove the shells from the broth with a slotted spoon and discard.

**3.** Add the lime juice, fish sauce, sliced ginger, red pepper flakes, sugar, mushrooms and shrimp to the pot, and cook for 3 minutes, or until the shrimp are cooked through. Remove from the heat and stir in the coconut milk and lime zest. To serve, spoon about ½ cup of the rice into each of 4 large soup bowls. Ladle the soup over the rice and serve immediately.

**Nutritional Analysis**
For each serving: 322 calories; 30 g. protein; 33 g. carbohydrates; 3 g. dietary fiber; 7.5 g. fat; 3.5 g. saturated fat; 172 mg. cholesterol, 2631 mg. sodium.

**SERVING SUGGESTION**
Serve with wilted spinach: In a large skillet, heat a small amount of olive oil and minced garlic over medium-high heat, about 1 minute. Place cleaned fresh spinach in the pan with only the water from rinsing clinging to its leaves. Toss the spinach as it cooks and remove the pan from the heat as soon as the leaves are wilted. Dress with a splash of low-sodium soy sauce, and add salt and pepper to taste.

# Shrimp, Bacon and Artichoke Pasta

It's amazing that such a decadent-tasting dinner as this one gets less than one-third of its calories from fat. Bacon is so strongly flavored that a little goes a long way, and by using a minimal amount of the drippings to cook the shrimp, that flavor goes even further.

## You Will Need

8 ounces farfalle
2 strips bacon
1 pound shrimp, peeled
1 (14-ounce) can artichoke hearts, drained and cut in ¼-inch strips
2 cloves garlic, thinly sliced
½ cup nonfat chicken broth
1 (7-ounce) jar roasted red peppers, chopped
¼ cup grated Parmesan cheese

**1.** Cook the pasta according to package instructions. Drain but do not rinse.

**2.** Meanwhile, cook the bacon in a skillet over medium-high heat. Remove the bacon from the pan and set aside. Wipe the pan with a paper towel, leaving just a thin film of bacon fat.

**3.** Add the shrimp and artichokes, and cook, stirring occasionally, about 3 minutes or until the shrimp are cooked through. Transfer to a large bowl.

**4.** Add the garlic to the skillet and cook over medium until soft, about 2 minutes. Add the chicken broth and cook 3 to 4 more minutes.

**5.** Crumble the bacon and add to the shrimp. Stir in the roasted peppers and the pasta. Add the garlic broth and toss thoroughly. Serve with the Parmesan cheese.

### Nutritional Analysis
For each serving: 499 calories; 41 g. protein; 48 g. carbohydrates; 2.1 g. dietary fiber; 14 g. fat; 5.1 g. saturated fat; 194 mg. cholesterol, 1099 mg. sodium.

### SERVING SUGGESTION
Serve with wilted greens: Cook fresh kale or mustard greens in a pot of boiling water until wilted and bright green. Drain in a colander. Add 1 tablespoon extra-virgin olive oil to the pot. Heat over medium high and add minced garlic and finely sliced red onion. Cook until the onions are soft and toss the greens back into the pot, cooking just until warm. Dress with a splash of balsamic vinegar.

**SERVES 4**

# Spanish Snapper

The combination of tomato, sweet pepper, onion and orange is what makes this dish reminiscent of Spanish flavors. Although it has a long ingredients list, this dish is really just a matter of chopping the green pepper and onion and pouring all the ingredients over the fish. You can easily prepare variations of this dish with flounder, sole or any other mild white fish.

## You Will Need

1½ pounds red snapper fillet
1 tablespoon extra-virgin olive oil
1 onion, chopped
1 green pepper, chopped
1 (14 ½-ounce) can whole plum
  tomatoes, drained and roughly chopped
½ teaspoon dried thyme
⅛ teaspoon red pepper flakes, or to taste
¼ cup white wine
¼ cup orange juice
½ teaspoon salt
¼ teaspoon black pepper
Orange zest for garnish

**1.** Preheat the oven to 400 degrees. Coat a baking dish large enough to hold the fish in a single layer with cooking spray. Place the fish in the baking dish.

**2.** In a bowl, combine the olive oil, onion, green pepper, tomatoes, thyme, red pepper flakes, white wine, orange juice, salt and pepper. Pour the mixture over the fish and bake about 15 minutes, or until fish is cooked through. Cut the fish into 4 pieces and serve with orange zest sprinkled over the top.

**Nutritional Analysis**
For each serving: 264 calories; 37 g. protein; 12 g. carbohydrates; 3 g. dietary fiber; 6 g. fat; 1 g. saturated fat; 63 mg. cholesterol, 555 mg. sodium.

**SERVING SUGGESTIONS**
Serve with saffron rice: Soak a couple of strands of saffron in 1 tablespoon hot tap water. Cook white rice according to package instructions, including the saffron water as part of the cooking water. Toss the rice with almond slivers and chopped parsley.

Also, serve sauteed Brussels sprouts: Heat extra-virgin olive oil over medium high. Add quartered Brussels sprouts and saute until lightly browned. Toss with lemon juice, salt and pepper.

**SERVES 4**

# Sauteed Salmon with Aromatic Tomato Topping

Cooking the tomato underneath the fish gives it additional flavor.
The fish finishes cooking slightly away from direct heat, which helps keep it moist. You can also use this method after searing chicken breasts or other types of fish.

## You Will Need

1 large or 2 small ripe tomatoes
  (¾ pound), chopped in ½-inch pieces
¼ teaspoon ground ginger
½ teaspoon ground cumin
1 teaspoon olive oil
1¼ pounds salmon fillet,
  cut in 4 pieces
1 tablespoon low-sodium soy sauce

**1.** Toss the tomatoes, ginger and cumin together and set aside.

**2.** Heat the olive oil in a skillet over medium high, and add the salmon, skin side down. After 2 minutes, drizzle the soy sauce over the fish. Cook 2 more minutes.

**3.** Add the tomato mixture and turn the salmon, allowing most of the tomato mixture to sit under the fish. Reduce the heat to low and cook for 5 more minutes, or until the salmon is still slightly translucent at its thickest point. To serve, spoon the tomatoes over each piece.

### Nutritional Analysis
For each serving: 234 calories; 30 g. protein; 5 g. carbohydrates; 1 g. dietary fiber; 10.5 g. fat; 1.6 g. saturated fat; 78 mg. cholesterol, 197 mg. sodium.

### SERVING SUGGESTIONS
Toast pignoli nuts in a dry skillet and toss while warm with extra-virgin olive oil, a pinch of sugar, salt and pepper. Toss with jasmine rice and chopped parsley.
Also, serve with steamed broccoli.

**SERVES 4**

# Kale and Kalamata-stuffed Sole

This dish should be baked in a dish you'll bring right to the table—it's very attractive and should be shown off. Use fresh kale for the best flavor.

## You Will Need

1 large bunch kale (about 1½ pounds)
12 kalamata olives, pitted
Zest from one lemon
1 (14½-ounce) can plum tomatoes, chopped in their juices
1½ pounds sole or flounder
⅓ cup white wine

**1.** Preheat the oven to 350 degrees.

**2.** Wash the kale but don't dry it. Bring 2 cups of water to a boil in a large saucepan. Add the kale and cook it until soft, tossing occasionally about 10 minutes. Drain it in a colander, squeeze out extra liquid, then chop it finely.

**3.** Mince the olives, then mix with the kale and lemon zest in a bowl.

**4.** Spread just enough of the tomatoes to cover the surface of a 9-by-13-inch baking dish. Lay each fillet out and cover it with 1 tablespoon of the tomatoes. Top with ¼ cup of the kale mixture, and starting with a short end roll the fillet up. Place it seam side down in the dish. Spoon the remaining tomatoes over the rolls and the remaining kale mixture in between the rolls. Drizzle the wine over the fish. Cover the baking dish with foil and bake for 20 minutes. Remove the foil and bake 5 more minutes, or until the fish is opaque. Serve immediately.

### Nutritional Analysis
For each serving: 277 calories; 36 g. protein; 16 g. carbohydrates; 3.3 g. dietary fiber; 5.9 g. fat; 1 g. saturated fat; 82 mg. cholesterol, 515 mg. sodium.

### SERVING SUGGESTION
Serve with a hash brown pancake: Saute frozen hash brown potatoes with diced green and red peppers, paprika, salt and black pepper. In the last minutes of cooking, spread potato mixture across skillet to form a large pancake. Turn the heat up, press the pancake down with the spatula, flip and repeat procedure. Cut into wedges and serve.

**Good Idea**

**QUICK START:**
White bean bruschetta: Cut a baguette into ½-inch slices and rub each slice with a cut clove of garlic. Lightly brush with olive oil and toast. In a food processor, combine ½ cup drained and rinsed white beans, 2 tablespoons extra-virgin olive oil and 2 garlic cloves. Add salt and pepper to taste. Puree. Stir in an additional ½ cup white beans. Top toasts with mixture.

# Savory Goat Cheese and Bacon Tart

This decadent dish is both elegant and rustic and makes an impressive presentation. While about half the calories come from fat, when served with the suggested bean soup, it is a nutritionally balanced meal.

## You Will Need
6 slices turkey bacon
1 ready-to-use unbaked pie crust (not in a pie plate)
2 ounces goat cheese
2 tablespoons plain nonfat yogurt
1 (14 ½-ounce) can sliced potatoes, drained
1 (7-ounce) jar roasted red peppers, drained

**1.** Preheat the oven to 425 degrees. Coat a cookie sheet with cooking spray.

**2.** Cook the bacon until lightly browned and crisp, about 5 minutes. Chop and set aside.

**3.** Working on a lightly floured surface, roll the dough into a 14- to 15-inch circle. Transfer to the cookie sheet.

**4.** Mix the goat cheese and yogurt in a small bowl and stir vigorously until softened and well-combined (there will still be lumps). Leaving a 2-inch border all around the pie crust, spread the mixture over the center of the dough, flattening some of the lumps with the back of a spoon.

**5.** Lay the potato slices on top of the cheese, sprinkle with the bacon, and top with the roasted pepper strips. Fold the empty 2-inch border in toward the center of the tart, forming overlapping pleats to keep a fairly round shape. Bake for 22 minutes, or until crust is golden brown.

### Nutritional Analysis
For each serving: 269 calories; 6 g. protein; 24 g. carbohydrates; 1.2 g. dietary fiber; 15 g. fat; 7 g. saturated fat; 29 mg. cholesterol, 653 mg. sodium.

### SERVING SUGGESTION
Serve with escarole and bean soup: Bring 1 (48-ounce) can nonfat chicken broth to a boil. Add 1 cup acini pepe or similar small pasta, return to a boil, and add 1 small head of escarole cut into 1-inch strips. Add ½ teaspoon each dried basil and thyme. When escarole is wilted and bright green, add 2 cans drained and rinsed white beans. Simmer for 5 minutes. Season to taste with salt and pepper.

**SERVES 6**

## About the Author

Marge Perry is a food journalist and cooking teacher who specializes in culinary lifestyle issues, such as stress-free entertaining and preparing healthful, interesting fare quickly.

Ms. Perry's newspaper work includes the nationally syndicated daily column, Dinner Tonight, written for Newsday, and restaurant reviews that appear regularly in The Bergen Record.

Ms. Perry is a contributing editor for Cooking Light, and writes for many other magazines, including Self, Weight Watchers Magazine, Mr. Food, InTouch and more. Her broadcast work includes her long-running weekly television segments on News12 — Meals in a Flash and At the Market. She is currently working on a second book on entertaining.

**Editor:** Kari Granville    **Assistant Editor:** E. Clarke Reilly

### Art

**Design Director:** Bob Eisner
**Art Director:** Joseph E. Baron
**Illustrations:** Steve Madden

### Photography

**Cover and Back Cover Author Photos:** Don Jacobsen
**Pantry:** Page 7, Bill Davis
**Chicken:** Page 13, J. Michael Dombroski
**Beef:** Page 45, Ken Spencer
**Fish:** Page 69, Bill Davis
**Pasta:** Page 97, Bill Davis
**Meatless:** Page 123, Ken Spencer
**Pizza:** Page 139, Bill Davis
**Guests:** Page 159, Bill Davis
**Food Styling:** Joanne Rubin

**Prepress:** Newsday Color Services
**Production:** Julian Stein